T0155587

Creating Game Environments in Blender 3D

Learn to Create Low Poly Game Environments

Ezra Thess Mendoza Guevarra

Apress®

Creating Game Environments in Blender 3D: Learn to Create Low Poly Game Environments

Ezra Thess Mendoza Guevarra
Laguna, Philippines

ISBN-13 (pbk): 978-1-4842-6173-6   ISBN-13 (electronic): 978-1-4842-6174-3
https://doi.org/10.1007/978-1-4842-6174-3

Managing Director, Apress Media LLC: Welmoed Spahr
Acquisitions Editor: Spandana Chatterjee
Development Editor: Matthew Moodie
Coordinating Editor: Divya Modi

Cover designed by eStudioCalamar

Cover image designed by Pixabay

Distributed to the book trade worldwide by Springer Science+Business Media New York, 1 New York Plaza, New York, NY 10004. Phone 1-800-SPRINGER, fax (201) 348-4505, e-mail orders-ny@springer-sbm.com, or visit www.springeronline.com. Apress Media, LLC is a California LLC and the sole member (owner) is Springer Science + Business Media Finance Inc (SSBM Finance Inc). SSBM Finance Inc is a **Delaware** corporation.

For information on translations, please e-mail booktranslations@springernature.com; for reprint, paperback, or audio rights, please e-mail bookpermissions@springernature.com.

Apress titles may be purchased in bulk for academic, corporate, or promotional use. eBook versions and licenses are also available for most titles. For more information, reference our Print and eBook Bulk Sales web page at http://www.apress.com/bulk-sales.

Any source code or other supplementary material referenced by the author in this book is available to readers on GitHub via the book's product page, located at www.apress.com/978-1-4842-6173-6. For more detailed information, please visit http://www.apress.com/source-code.

Printed on acid-free paper

To Father God.
To my mother and father.
To my fellow Filipinos.
To my relatives and friends.
To all PWDs (especially Epileptic).

Table of Contents

About the Author

Ezra Thess Mendoza Guevarra graduated with a bachelor of science degree in information technology from STI College, the Philippines. Though she's become a web developer, her passion for the arts, which started in her childhood, never went away. In 2016, she became interested in 3D modeling. Ezra is the administrator of the website `www.didyouknow45.wordpress.com` through which she shares her research.

Despite being epileptic, she continues to pursue her dreams and "break the walls." A researcher and passionate artist, Ezra is currently using her skills as a freelancer.

About the Technical Reviewer

 **Mieren Taylor** is a 3D generalist who works with independents and small businesses to create product visuals and promotional material, as well as patching pipelines in various productions. Some of the projects she has worked on include making product assets for JOV Photo Lab, 3D Sarees for Yes!Poho; creating 3D visuals for Kairma Air filters, and many more. She has been working with Blender as a freelancer for 5+ years and has every intention to carry on using this amazing software and exploring the new features of its latest version for all new projects.

You can see Mieren's latest work on her website `www.Tomations.com`.

Acknowledgments

First of all, I'd like to thank my dear readers for purchasing my second book. Of course, without you, this book's purpose will just be in vain.

I'd also like to thank the efforts of all the staff who worked with this book. Despite being in a pandemic, you guys were able to work hard on this book. I don't know all of you, but of course, you know who you are.

Of course, thank you Ms. Spandana Chaterjee, Ms. Divya Modi, Mr. Matthew Moodie, and Ms. Mieren Taylor for your assistance, effort, and patience. Thanks for everything.

Thank you to my dearest mother, Cecilia Guevarra; and dearest father, Alexander Guevarra, for your support on everything.

Thank you to my HIJCC family who always pray for every member. Thank you also to my friends and previous employers who have given me memories and necessary experiences.

Of course, I will always thank my number one partner here, Father God, who always gives me strength and wisdom. Thanks for everything.

Introduction

Good day my dear reader! Wherever you are coming from, whatever time you are reading this book of mine, I'd like to greet you and say, "Welcome to the world of 3D game!"

Game is something that is been enjoyed by anyone. Whatever gender you are, whatever age you are, wherever country you came from, there is always a chance you have already played a game. It's just that now, many games are already digital.

From physical games to digital, from pixel or 2D to 3D, games already have a long history. They have even developed lots of genres and types along the way.

We are now in a time that most of the games developed are in 3D. Even the past popular games like Mario Brothers have been adopted to 3D for the new era.

But creating a game is divided into two parts: designing and development. In this book, we will discuss the designing part.

In this book, we will talk about how to create a basic 3D game environment using Blender 3D – from modeling, to texturing, and adding lighting.

So, let's start learning end I hope you enjoy this book!

CHAPTER 1

Getting Started

Good day, dear readers! Welcome to Chapter 1 of my book, which is about getting started creating game environments in Blender 3D.

Here we're going to talk about what exactly a game environment is, the role of a game environment, and the skills needed to make it in this field. We're going to talk about some tools that will be able to speed up the process, too, in creating your project with Blender.

So, that's enough for our introduction – let's get started.

Game Environment

Igi-global.com defines a game environment as being a dimension that brings game rules, objectives, subjects, and theoretical aspects together as a whole to provide an interactive flow of activity.

This means that a game environment isn't just the appearance or the graphics that you can see in the game. When you say game environment, it involves the rules, purpose, and target – meaning the whole mood of the game.

You might also encounter the word **level design** and be confused between the two, as I used to be. **Level design** is about the challenges that the player will encounter in the game while **game environment** is about the aesthetics, architectural design, and mood you will create in the game.

In game design, you should be able to convey your feelings to your target audience or player.

Note "Environmental design establishes the world." – Josh Byser, Level Design vs. Environmental Design at Medium.com

---

© Ezra Thess Mendoza Guevarra 2020
E. T. Mendoza Guevarra, *Creating Game Environments in Blender 3D*,
https://doi.org/10.1007/978-1-4842-6174-3_1

Game Environment Artist

Let's now proceed to discuss the role of an environment artist, as well as the skills and tools needed for this position.

A game environment artist is the one who creates the world of the game. For example, if you create a game with a cooking simulation theme, he or she is the one who will create the restaurant feel with vibrant color. Ah! Don't be confused when you see the term **prop artist**. In the given example theme, restaurant game, a prop artist is the one in charge of creating the *game assets* like dishes, chairs, etc., but the position of prop artist depends on the studio. Their jobs can also be done by a game environment artist. In other words, it means creating game assets that pertain to every object that can be seen in the games; creating game rules; creating a game system that is the flow of the game; and creating a game concept, which is the idea of the game or the story of the game and all fall under the game environment artist role. But depending on the studio you are working with, you can divide it into different to increase efficiency in each area. For example, if you hire someone for concept art only, you can create a concept for a game that can attract many target users. This is usually done by big studios to create an outstanding game while some indie game studios only assign that listed role to one or two artists because of a lack of budget; and in some indie studios, they will hire artists and randomly assign tasks based on what the artist can do.

Game Environment Artists' Skills

So now, let's talk about the skills necessary for a game environment artist. According to Robert Hodri, a senior 3D artist and environment artist at Id Software in his article at Arstation.com, having a passion for video games and art in general would be a plus for a game artist.[1] I'd like to add, if you have the passion, then working with games will not be work for you, but rather play since that's what you love, though this isn't required by companies.

Since those who create a game environment or game assets are also called artists, **creativity skills** are obviously present. Don't worry, everyone is born with creative skills. It just so happens that not everyone has been able to harness this skill of theirs as they grow. Just like communication skills, creative skills must be trained as you grow up so they will not be lost. If you ever feel that you have already lost them, don't worry. You can bring them back by practicing again with them.

---

[1]https://magazine.artstation.com/2017/03/game-environment-artist/

Next to creative skills are **communication skills**. There will be a time that you will communicate with different types of people. Without this type of skill, you might fail to deliver your idea to your team. You also need to have the ability to work independently because there are times that you will work alone. So, in other words, you should be **flexible**. This means that you can easily adapt to what the projects need.

Communication skills are one big asset. The flexibility to easily adapt to sudden changes in plans and time management are also essential, especially if you have other things that you're doing aside from creating games. Also important is decision-making. You need to learn to decide when to say **yes** and when to say **no**. I guess you don't want to die before your game get sick in the market, right? It's just a joke but to remind you to think of your health, too, and not just sit in front of a computer 24 hours a day and drink coffee. You need to learn patience also. Yeah, patience is a skill now!

As you probably notice, I discuss more about soft skills rather than technical skills. Remember, technical skills can easily be learned, but soft skills need to become habit before they become part of you.

Game Assets

Game Assets. I already gave a sneak peek of game assets, but what exactly are game assets? Game assets are anything that is part of the game: objects, scenes, materials or textures, lighting – everything is called game assets.

Essential Technical Skills

Let's talk about the technical skills that could help you increase your productivity in creating a game environment.

Since we're creating a game, number one on the list is the game engines. Learning the game engines will help you know how your props or assets will be implemented. We have tons of game engines around here nowadays. Popular ones are Unity3D, Unreal Engine, and CryEngine. We also have open source game engines like UPBGE and Armory3D. They are both a base in Blender, so making a game asset from Blender and importing it to these two will not be hard.

If you already want to create more outstanding textures and materials, Photoshop and Substance Painter are there to assist you. These two software are capable of helping you to create more creative texture since they have features that are specifically for that part. Blender has its own features that can be found in texture workspaces, but I will also introduce these to you so you can have options.

Although Blender also has its features for sculpting that can be found in the Sculpting workspace, I'd like to introduce to you these two: Zbrush and 3D Coat. If you want to create more stunning assets where you need to sculpt, like in characters, you can use them.

Just take note that Photoshop, Substance Painter, Zbrush, and 3D Coat are all paid software. If you want a free one aside from Blender that you can try on, here are some:

- Gimp is a free open source software that is known to be an alternative to Photoshop but I can say that in order to create texture and materials here, it's not an easy task unless you have already mastered this software.

- SculptGL is a free web application that is an alternative to Zbrush and 3D coat. You can visit it here: `https://stephaneginier.com/sculptgl/` and since it was a web application, you can't use it without internet but I like it as an alternative one. It's easy to use.

Well, the above list contains options for you, but this book will focus on creating game environments with Blender3D. So, in the end, we will be with Blender 3D.

Types of Games

We also need to know the different types of games before we start creating a game so we will know what type of game we will create, who will be our target, etc.

In general, we have three main types of games: Party Games, Tabletop Games, and Video Games.

When it comes to video games, we also have different genres. These include:

- Action-Adventure games: A combination of core elements of action and adventure.

- Adventure games: Where its main elements are focused on an adventure theme.

- Escape games: They are a kind of game with settings of a locked room and you will find a clue on how to escape from it. It's a sub-genre of adventure games.

- First Person Shooter (FPS): This is a game that is centered in a weapon-based combat in a first-person perspective. The player sees the game through the eyes of the main character of the game.

- Third Person Shooter: Here, the player can see the game in a third-person perspective. This is a game where you can see the main character fight and move rather than see what's the perspective of the main character.

- Multiplayer online battle arena: A sub-genre of strategy games. For the best description, think *Dota 2* and *League of Legends*. Yeah. Those kinds of games where there are players teaming up, creating two teams to fight against each other online.

- Platform games: This is a sub-genre of action games. This type of genre focuses on games where the player must jump or climb to avoid obstacles in the suspended platforms. Its features often involve uneven terrain that has different heights.

- Real-time strategy games: This is another sub-genre of strategy games. In this game, the two players will protect their assets by constructing new assets/units or destroying the other player's assets/units.

- Role-Playing video games (RPG): This is where the player controls the main character of the game toward a certain goal in its game world. *Legend of Mana* and *Pokémon* are some good examples.

- Simulation games: This type of game is created to simulate a real-life scene.

- Sports games: Games where its main elements are focused on sports themes.

- Casual games: Games with simpler rules, simple gameplay, and shorter sessions. It's usually targeted to the masses more than a specific audience like the other genres.

- Flash games: Games that you can play in the browser. They are usually made with HTML5, CSS, and JavaScript. But now, there are also some game engines that can help you easily create web-based games like Godot Engine.

- Mini games: These are the small games usually included inside a video game. You can call this a bonus game or side game.

- Alternate reality games: These are the kinds of games in which the main platform is the real world while the player gets instructions from different forms of media. For example, someone sends a fax of page 1 of a manuscript or novel that is soon to be published. Some may reject it because it was just a piece of paper, but some notice that there is an anomaly in the words and try to decode it, search it, and see that there are instructions in it indicating what to do next and so on. A real-life example of this was the game *Year Zero*.[2] There are no announcements about the game. For players to be able to participate, they must realize that on the back of the Nine Inch Nail 2007 European tour shirt, there is a code that will reveal the word **I am trying to believe** and after they search it, they get this website – IAmTryingToBelieve.com – about strange phenomenon and the game continues.

- Augmented reality games: Pokémon Go. Yes. If you played Pokémon Go, you know how these kinds of games work; but okay, I'll also explain. This kind of game is like a mix of the real world and virtual world.

There's a lot of types of games around here nowadays. As technology evolves, games evolve too. There might be some types that I'm not able to list, but at least we have some here and can consider them as we can think about when we start to create a game.

---

[2]Extra Credits: ARGs https://www.youtube.com/watch?v=tiU4AYPdIOw

Low Poly vs. High Poly?

Low Poly vs. High Poly? There's a lot of this question on the internet, but is there really such a thing as **low poly vs. high poly**? Okay. Let's start by defining each term.

The word poly comes from the word polygon, which is a two-dimensional shape made of straight lines and angles. In mathematics, a polygon is a closed shape where the sides are all in line segments, and each side must intersect with exactly two other sides but only at their endpoints. We also have different types of polygons, and they are named based on how many sides they have. In Blender 3D, polygons are shapes with three or more sides defined by three-dimensional points called vertices, connected by lines called edges; and the interior region of the polygon is called faces.

Polygons, in theory, can have any number of sides but are commonly broken down into triangles for display. In general, the more triangles in a mesh, the more detailed the object is and becomes high poly but becomes harder for the computer to display it. In order for you to optimize the whole scene, the number of triangles in the scene must be reduced, by using low poly meshes.

What is the basis if one object is a low poly or a high poly? Well, the answer is unknown. What? Unknown? Well, not exactly unknown – just like there is no explanation for it. What I mean with this is there is no definite basis if one object is low poly or high poly. An object will be called low poly or high poly depending on the poly count or number of polygons used in your game asset in relation to first, its target hardware; second, the kind of game you will create; third, the position of the game assets in your game environment; and fourth, the hardware you will use in creating your game. Let me explain it further.

The game Super Mario 64 is considered low poly at this time, but during its release, it was a major achievement. This is because as time passes by, technology advances and standards in the design also become higher than before. This is why what we called high poly before is low poly now.

Both high poly and low poly have their own parts. High poly is important to achieve a detailed surface while low poly is important for game engines, subdivision modeling, and low-polygon proxy geometries of high poly ones for rigging and animation. It's just that both of them have their own consequences when you use them.

When it comes to high poly, the problem lies in controlling an enormous amount of vertices, maybe from sculpting, subdivision surfaces made in low poly, curves or nurbs surfaces, or generated by 3D scanning etc., while in low poly, the polygons' problems lie in topology, which has to follow some rules so that the shading looks right.

In creating a game, you will not just create a game base on a one-sided computer specification, right? For example, I create an RPG game. It's not enough that I create an interesting design. It's not enough that I create interesting game play. It's not enough that I create an interesting game concept. I should think about how my target audience will be able to play my game. If every part of my game is very detailed like how you see in movies like *Jumanji*, will a computer with 4GB RAM be able to handle it? Will a cellphone with 2gb RAM be able to handle it? Oh, come on. Don't laugh. Those specs still exist. There are those who are still using Windows XP service pack 2 thinking it is the safest Windows version among all. So you need to know your target market and your target market's ability when you create your game so that your effort will not be wasted.

Another thing: when you compare the high poly assets created in a game in high poly models used in films, obviously the one used in a game will be called low poly compared to the other. This is why some said low poly and high poly are relative terms. This means that it really depends on the usage of the model and when the model is created.

What's the point of the previous examples? First, we don't have an exact poly count that we will say is the maximum number of low poly or a minimum number for high poly. No. We don't have that. Second, you need both low poly and high poly. When creating a game, you want some parts to be emphasized and look better, especially the part that is close to the screen. But since we're thinking of making the game lighter, you can use low poly in some parts of the game that are not that close to the screen. What do I mean by this? It's the level of detail. To look good close up, degrade those in the background.

There are many techniques created in order to use low poly and high poly in a game efficiently without making it harder for computers, and here are some of those:

- You can convert low poly to high poly by using MultiRes modifiers to sculpt high poly while retaining low poly geometry.

- You can convert high poly to low poly through Retoplogy or decimation, and the details from high poly can be baked into texture maps.

- For textures on low poly, you want them two times larger than a texture that has same size on a model as pixels on screen because of the so-called **texture filtering**.

- For high poly, you want polygons small enough so that the surface detail will be well defined.

- Use normal or bump mapping by making a low poly object appear to contain more detail than it does.

Okay, what is this texture filtering? Texture filtering deals with how a texture or the 2D image is displayed in 3D. It takes data of the texture – for example, its color – to improve the quality of the texture that will be displayed on the screen.

Let's discuss some kinds of texture filtering:

- Bilinear Filtering is the simplest method of texture filtering. When pixels fall between texels or textured, it samples the four nearest texels to find its color.

- Trilinear Filtering smooths the transition between **mipmaps** by taking samples from both.

- Anisotropic Filtering (AF) significantly improves texture quality at oblique angles. When you look at a snapshot of a 3D game with an AF off and a snapshot with AF on, you will see how the texture, especially in grounds, becomes more detailed and even improves its colors of some game assets. It has 2x, 4x, 8x, and 16x flavors. This refers to the steepness of the angle the filtering is applied to.

Let's have a little side note before I end up this section.

What are Mipmaps? Mipmaps are smaller, pre-filtered versions of a texture image, representing different levels of detail of the texture. They are often stored in sequences and progressively smaller textures called mipmap chains, with each level half smaller compared to the previous one. It is used for situations when the distance of the object and the camera can be changed. As the object become far away from the camera, the texture or texel become smaller and smaller. The textures will have to be scaled down in the process called minification filtering. The problem with this method is when you need to sample the entire texture at runtime for an object that can only be a single pixel wide.

This is the purpose of mipmaps. Instead of sampling just a single texture, the application can be set up to switch between any of the lower resolution mipmaps in the chain, depending on the distance from the camera.

The use of mipmaps can improve the image quality by eliminating aliasing effects caused by oversampling textures, and they can also improve performance because they increase cache efficiency and as full-size textures will not be needed as often, the lower resolution mipmaps will fit more easily in the texture cache.

Blender's Installation Process

First of all, of course you need to download it from its website `www.blender.org`. I'd like to make a note that if you want to download other versions, like the older one, rather than clicking the button in the header of the site that says Download Blender, you can go and click the Download tab ➤ go to the part of the page where it says "Go experimental" and click "Get Blender Experimental." Here, you can see all the Blender versions from the oldest.

You also have two options when downloading a Blender release. You can see it in the download page, under the MacOS, Linux, and other versions drop menu. Here you can see that Blender has an .exe file and a portable file for Windows.

For Windows: when you install the .exe file, you just only need to right-click and open or run it and follow the direction of the installation setup, unless you have modifications you wanted to do in its installation: for example, for the drive that will be installed, you can click the **advance** option and follow the steps. When installing the zip or portable file, you just need to extract it with the software you have: for example, WinZip or WinRAR.

For MacOs: when you install the dmg (disk-images) file, double-click it and then drag **Blender.app** into the application folders. When you install using the zip file, extract it and drag the **Blender.app** into the applications folder.

For Linux: when you install from Package Manager, I'd like to note that some Linux distribution may have a specific package for Blender in their repositories. Installing Blender via the distribution's native mechanism ensures consistency with other packages on the system. Be aware, too, that the package may be outdated compared to the latest official release. When you install from Blender.org, download the Linux version for your architecture and extract it to the desired location.

For more about the installation process, you can visit `docs.blender.org/manual/ en/latest/getting_started/installing/index.html`.

So, this is the end of Chapter 1. I hope you learned something in this chapter. In the next chapter, we will discuss the first part of creating a game environment using Blender. I'll be using Blender 2.82 when demonstrating the project.

CHAPTER 2

Let's Create!

Good day, dear readers! Now we're here at Chapter 2 of our book. This chapter covers the topics related to modeling tools and features of Blender. I'll also be discussing a bit about some basic stuff for beginners of Blender so they can follow along without difficulty.

So, let's get started!

Blender Preferences

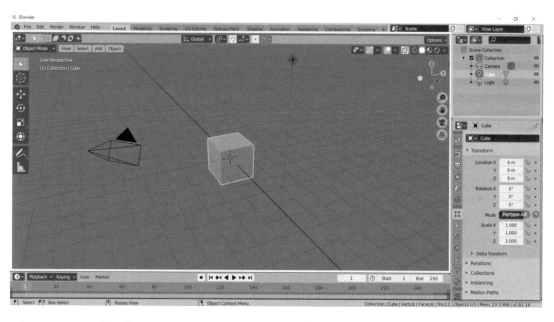

Figure 2-1. *Blender 2.82: Layout Workspace(Red:Tool Setting; Yellow:3D viewport, Orange:Properties;Green: Outliner)*

In Blender 2.80, the default color of the interface is dark with colored icons; and for Blender 2.82 (Figure 2-1), the color is light gray. But don't worry, guys! If you want to use the theme from 2.80 instead of 2.82, you can just go to edit ➤ preferences ➤ themes ➤ and go to the select menu, as shown in Figure 2-2, and choose Blender Dark.

© Ezra Thess Mendoza Guevarra 2020
E. T. Mendoza Guevarra, *Creating Game Environments in Blender 3D*,
https://doi.org/10.1007/978-1-4842-6174-3_2

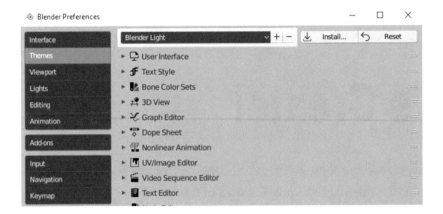

Figure 2-2. *Blender Preferences*

This Blender Preference appears as a new small window after you click **preference** in the **edit menu**. You can also add your own edited theme here by clicking the plus icon beside the select menu and deleting an existing theme by clicking the minus icon.

Now let's discuss one of the basic things that we need to review before digging into an advanced lesson: workspaces.

Workspaces

Workspaces are essentially predefined window layouts. You can also create your own workspaces by clicking the plus icon beside the sculpting workspace tab. Workspaces help you create your project with ease since they are already set up for different projects like modeling, animating, sculpting, texturing, shading, rendering, etc. For this chapter, since our focus will be on modeling, I will discuss the layout workspace and modeling workspace, which are both helpful in modeling aspects.

Take a look at Figures 2-3 and 2-4 to see the look of layout workspace and modeling workspace.

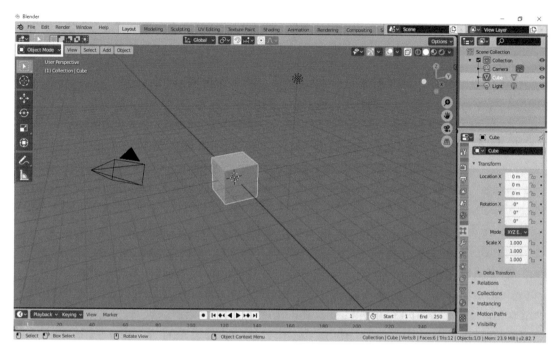

Figure 2-3. *Layout Workspace*

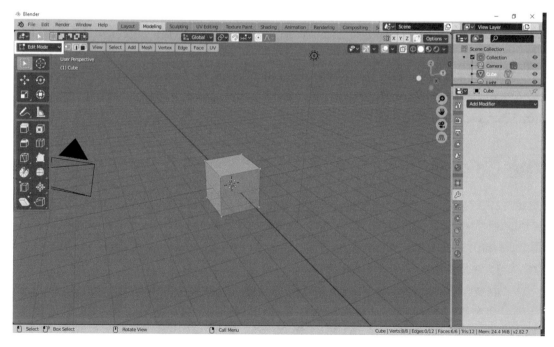

Figure 2-4. *Modeling Workspace*

You can see that I put a rectangle in the four parts of both workspaces. These four parts will be used the most so I want to at least give you an overview of these four. The first one, the one in the yellow rectangle, is the select menu for modes. These modes change the setup of the 3D viewport (the large area where you saw your object), to help you easily apply your ideas. The one in the red rectangle is the toolbox where, of course, your main tools can be found. We will discuss more about it soon so just sit tight. The one in the blue rectangle is the outliner where you can see your objects listed. You can change their names through the outliner or even delete the object, just like how you can change your layer name or delete your layer in Photoshop. I'm sure you know how to use Photoshop. What? You don't know? Okay then, as you can see, beside the orange icon, there are names like cube, camera, and light, right? If you double-click it using the left mouse button (*or left touch pad button for laptop users*), you will see the name highlighted, a sign that you can already change its name. If you do a right-click using your mouse button (*or right touch pad button for laptop users*), a drop menu will pop up that contains a selection for copying or deleting the selected object.

You can also hide the object in the viewport by toggling the eye icon beside the name. You also hide it in the rendering process by toggling the camera icon, which by default isn't enabled in outliner. You can enable it in the filter select menu, which is beside the search menu that can be found at the top part of the outliner.

By default, some parts of the outliner can't be seen – the same with others like the toolbox and properties windows. You can adjust it by placing your cursor in the side (not in the edge) and dragging it.

Now we have two things needed in order to proceed in modeling: our 3D objects and our 3D modeling toolbox (I'm talking about the features of software specific to modeling stuff). Let's start by discussing the objects.

The Objects

First of all, we need to know the objects present before we start modeling. There's a lot of different types of objects in Blender, and not all of them can be edited for modeling. Objects have their own purposes, just like a paper and a pen. Some of them are just for creating a scene, like the lights and camera.

Let's discuss the types of objects that Blender has so we will know its limits and capabilities; but before that, there are two ways of adding objects. The first way is to go to add menu ➤ and choose from the listed objects, and the other way is to hold **Shift + A** and choose from the listed options.

Mesh Objects

Take a look at Figures 2-5 and 2-6 so you can see the list of mesh objects.

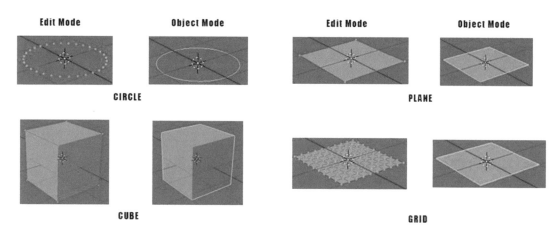

Figure 2-5. *From the top left: Circle, Plane, Cube, and Grid*

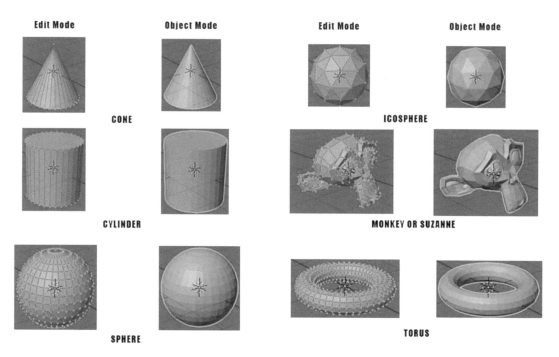

Figure 2-6. *From the top left: Cone, Icosphere, Cylinder, Monkey, Sphere, Torus*

What we have here are the following: Circle, Plane, Cube, Grid, Cone, Icosphere, Cylinder, Monkey or previously called Suzanne, Sphere, and Torus.

For our object circle, you can notice that when you look at it in object mode, it looks like just a thin circle line, which is similar to curve objects; but when you look it in edit mode, what you can see are vertices or dots, connecting a line or called edges, to form a circle.

This is how mesh objects are composed. Meshes are composed of **vertices,** which are the dots highlighted in orange that you can see in the edit mode, **edges** are the lines that form a face and **faces**, which are a the triangles or squares that form a mesh object.

In the case of a **circle mesh object**, it only has vertices and edges.

You can also notice that the plane and the grid have the same look when you view it in the object mode, but you can see its difference in edit mode.

Grid mesh object, unlike plane, is already divided in nine columns and nine rows. It was like a subdivided plane, ready for some basic modeling, like modeling a leaf.

So, what are the object mode and edit mode? Blender has six modes available for mesh objects that can help you ease your modeling process: Object mode, Edit mode, Sculpt mode, Vertex Paint, Weight, Paint, and Texture Paint. In object mode, you can do general modeling like scaling the object and rotating while in edit mode, you can do more modeling like transforming a mesh object from its ordinary form to another form. Take a look at Figure 2-7 to see an example of the differences between these two modes in their functions.

Object Mode

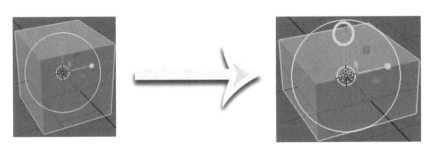

Edit Mode

Figure 2-7. *Scaling Object mode and Edit mode*

I use both of the Z-axes in scaling the cube. As you can see in our example in Figure 2-8, when you transform an object in object mode, you transform an object as a whole, but when you transform an object in edit mode, you do it by parts of an object (like vertices, edges, and faces).

I'd like to note that these modes are not only for mesh objects. They are also available in other objects, and other objects like armatures have their own modes.

Now let's proceed to other objects.

Curve Objects

Curve objects are defined by control points and have two modes: object mode and edit mode. Take a look at Figure 2-8 to see the list of these types of objects.

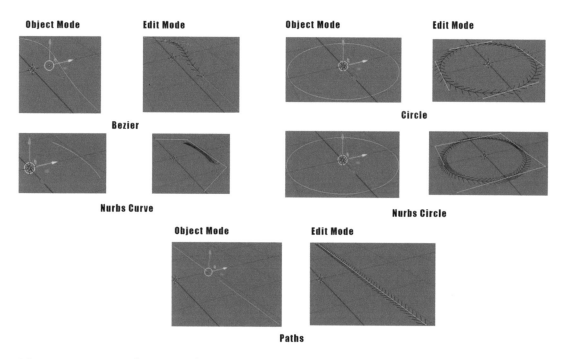

Figure 2-8. *List of Curve Objects*

As you can see in Figure 2-8, the circle in curve objects is the same in circle that you can see in mesh objects when you view it in object mode. You can also notice that the circle and nurbs circle here in curve objects look the same in object mode, but you can see its difference in edit mode, how its control points have been structured. It's the same for the path. You might notice that in object mode, it looks like just a thin line but in edit mode, you can already notice its control points.

Take a look at Figure 2-9 to see how the control points of the curve objects work.

Figure 2-9. *Nurbs Circle transformed into heart shape*

Control points can help you easily transform the curve objects into the shapes you want to create, curve objects especially can be converted to mesh objects by the following steps:

In object mode, left-click (or right-click if your default was changed to right-click) on the curve object or in any space in the 3D viewport like you see in Figure 2-10.

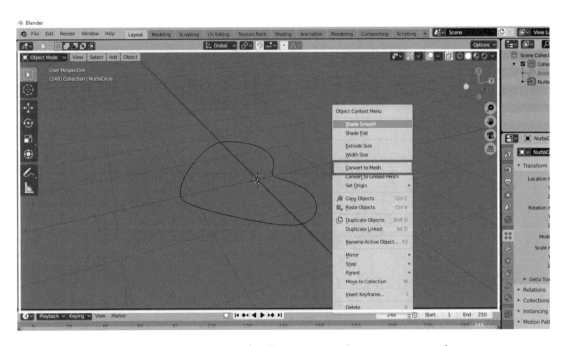

Figure 2-10. *Object Context Menu (Yellow rectangle: 3D viewport)*

Then, click the convert to mesh and you will see a change of icon in the outliner, which you can see at the top-right corner of your window, which will indicate that your curve object already converted to a mesh object. Take a look at Figure 2-11 to see these icons.

Figure 2-11. *Convert to Mesh Icon in Outliner*

For some, a curve object cannot easily seen in the viewport under object mode because it was just like a thin line. But when you go to the edit mode, you can see vertices that represents the curve object that currently active and you can modify it at the same time, as you can see in Figure 2-12.

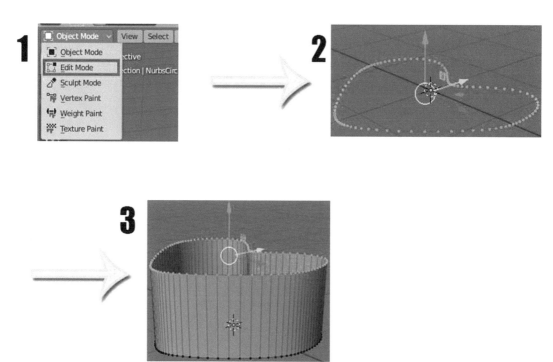

Figure 2-12. *Modifying the Mesh converted from Curve object*

So, from edit mode, I press "**A**" to highlight all the vertices of the object and extrude it by pressing **E** in the keyboard. You can also highlight the vertices/edges/faces/objects by clicking the Select Box, Select Circle, or Select Lasso from the toolbar as you can see in Figure 2-13.

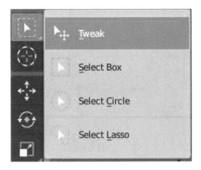

Figure 2-13. *Select Tools*

You can find these tools in both object and edit modes. In order for you to see these drop-downs, you need to hold click on the Select icon as shown in Figure 2-13. You can also access these tools by its shortcut keys: press **B** for Select Box, **C** for Select Circle, and **L** for Select Lasso.

We have different extruding tools in Blender, but we will discuss them separately. For now, let's focus on the objects.

Let's now proceed to surface objects.

Surface Objects

Surface objects are also defined by control points and only have two modes: object and edit, but when it comes to its control points, their effect is quite different than in the curve objects. Surface objects have a few options and tools for editing too, unlike the curve objects. Take a look at Figure 2-14 to see the list of these object types.

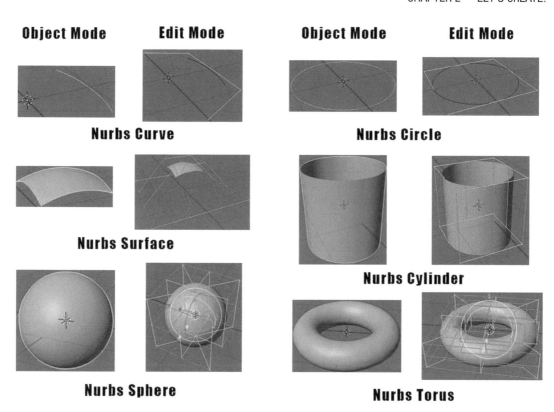

Object Mode   **Edit Mode**   **Object Mode**   **Edit Mode**

Nurbs Curve   **Nurbs Circle**

Nurbs Surface   **Nurbs Cylinder**

Nurbs Sphere   **Nurbs Torus**

Figure 2-14. *List of Surface Objects*

Just like the curve objects, you can convert the surface object to a mesh object in object mode by going to **Object menu ➤ Convert to ➤ Mesh from Curve/Meta/Surf/Text**. Now, take a look at Figures 2-15 and 2-16 in order to see how you can modify a surface object.

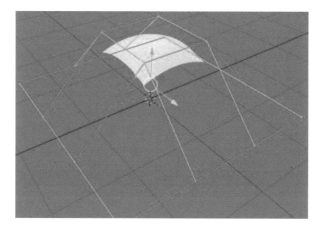

Figure 2-15. *Nurbs Surface in Edit Mode (Layout Workspace)*

21

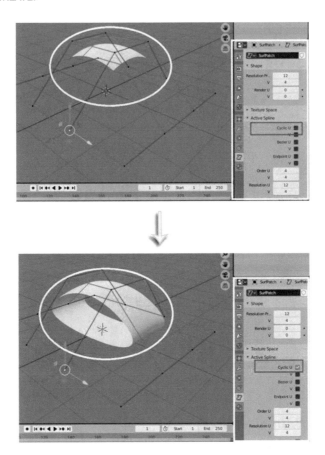

Figure 2-16. *Nurbs Surface modified*

As you can see in Figure 2-16, I modify the Nurbs surface by simply toggling something from the properties, which is the one in the yellow rectangle. In the case of Nurbs surface, I toggle **Cyclic U** in the object data panel for the surface to be closed. The U and the V indicated axes for 2D objects like surfaces so you can control them independently. Take a look at Figure 2-17 to see a basic example of what we can do with a surface object.

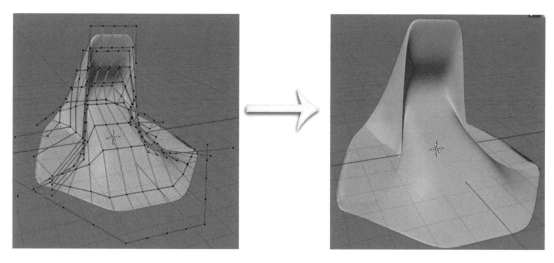

Figure 2-17. *Nurbs Surface sample output after modified*

You might wonder how come in Figure 2-17, I have many segments or control points in the edit mode compared to previous figures. During the process, I subdivide the segments by going to **Segments menu ➤ Subdivide**, and it will subdivide the current selected segment/s. What I do to accomplish the abstract model is just by subdividing the segments three times and then scaling and moving the control points.

So now, let's proceed to the next type of object, which is the metaball.

Metaballs Objects

A metaball, in my opinion, is quite complicated to use. The moment the two metaballs touch or get close to each other, they merge. Unlike our previous examples, metaballs are not defined by vertices (unlike meshes) and not by control points (unlike surfaces and curves). They are defined by a mathematical formula that is calculated by Blender. You can turn this to a mesh object, just like curve and surface, by going to **Object Menu ➤ Convert To ➤ Mesh from Meta/Curve/Surf/Text.** Metaballs have two modes: object mode and edit mode.

Figure 2-18 shows a list of metaballs.

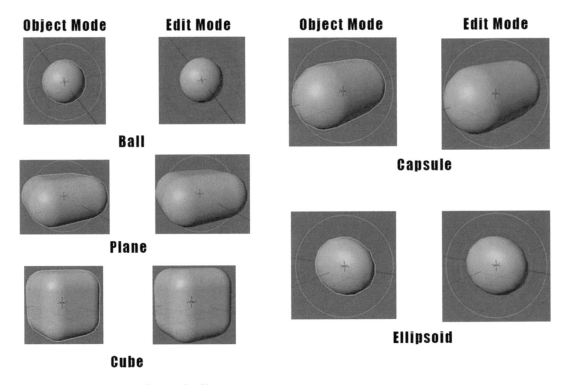

Figure 2-18. *List of Metaballs*

As you can notice, when in object mode, you can see one ring around the metaballs; while in edit mode, you can see two rings except in cube. You cannot see a ring, whether you're in object mode or in edit mode. Well, when it comes to cube, its ring is hidden unless you edit something in edit mode, and then you will see these two rings appear. Okay. What are these rings for?

The ring that you can see in the object mode and the outside ring in the edit mode are called selection rings while the inner ring in the edit mode is called influence, which has direct control of the metaball's stiffness.

You can also use metaballs for modeling like to form an initial shape of your model, streams, or water droplets.

Since metaballs can easily merge or blend to each other, they often work as a family of objects or groups. When it comes to this, you must know that there are already two or three **metas (shortcut for metaball)** merged together; the base meta is the one who determines the transformation, and resolution has the materials and textures or acts like a parent for the other metas. In order to determine which is the base meta, the one in which its object name is without a number, for example, we have the following: Mball, Mball.001, Mball.002; Mball is the base meta of the metaballs.

In order for me to explain more about metaballs, take a look at Figures 2-19 and 2-20.

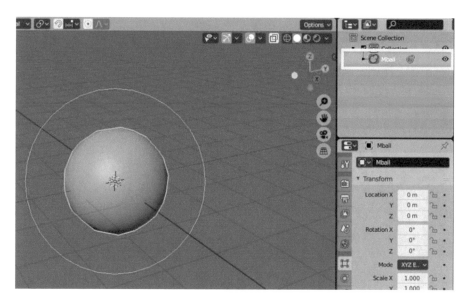

Figure 2-19. *Adding the first metaball*

You can notice that in our outliner, the first meta has the name Mball.

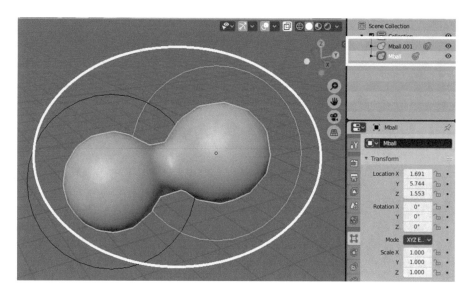

Figure 2-20. *Adding the next metaball*

As you can see, after I add the next meta named Mball.001 and make the two touch each other, when I select the base meta, which is the Mball, it selected the one present in our 3D viewport. But you might also notice that it didn't highlight the selection ring for the other meta. Let's try to delete the selected one and see in Figure 2-21 what will happen.

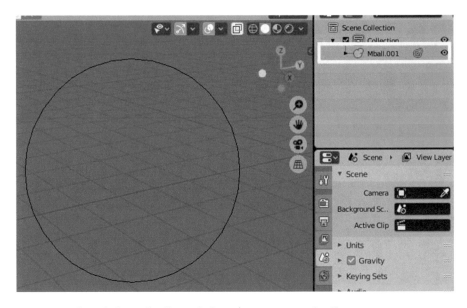

Figure 2-21. *Deleted the Mball and the remaining Mball.001*

Eh? What happened? Mball.001 remained with only a ring? Now, take a look at Figure 2-22 for more about this.

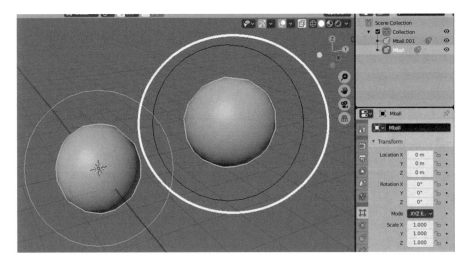

Figure 2-22. *Added new metaball*

As I add a new metaball while the ring is in there, you can see that it automatically adds two metaballs. You can think of the rings around the metaballs as a container. If you want to delete the metas because you want to make some changes but you want to add them again, with the same number, just leave the rings there and add metaballs and voila! You will add a number of metaballs easily.

Now, let's move on to the next object, which is the Text object.

Text Objects

Text objects are objects in Blender to create text. They have two modes: object mode and the edit mode. You can edit the default text of this object in the edit mode only. You can turn this object to mesh just like the curve, surface, and metaballs by going to **Object Menu ➤ Convert To ➤ Mesh from Meta/Curve/Surf/Text** and convert this to a curve object by going to **Object Menu ➤ Convert To ➤ Curve from Mesh/Text**.

Take a look at Figure 2-23 to see the actual view of a text object.

Figure 2-23. *Text Object viewed in two modes*

The one inside the red rectangle is the cursor, just like when you are typing in a regular document. In editing its fonts, I do it in the object data panel that can be found in the properties section.

Now, let's proceed to the next object, which are the grease pencil objects.

Grease Pencil Objects

These are objects that can help you for your 2D ideas. Yes, 2D since you can already create a 2D scene or 2D animation in Blender. But depending on you, you can also use this for character modeling or even in designing game assets or game environments. These objects serve as a container of strokes that allow you to draw in a 3D space. These objects have five modes: Object mode, Edit mode, Sculpt mode, Draw mode, and Weight Paint mode.

Take a look at Figure 2-24 to see the list of grease pencil objects.

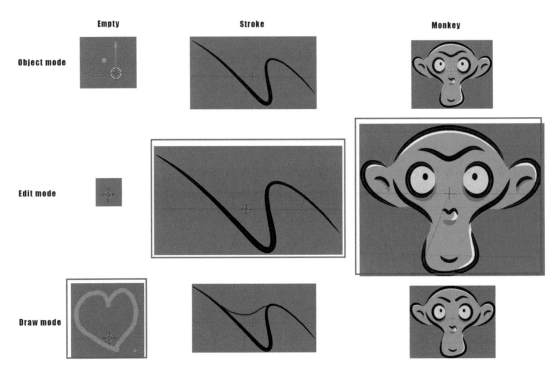

Figure 2-24. *List of Grease Pencil Objects*

In empty object, if you look at it in both object mode and edit mode, by default, you can see it as literally an empty object. It shows our definition of a grease pencil, an object that serves as a container for strokes since when you go to draw mode and draw something on it, that's the time you can see something in the empty object unlike in the stroke object and monkey object. But wait, if you notice in Figure 2-24, for the stroke and monkey, you can see a line inside the black stroke of the two objects.

Let's take a closer look at the line in Figure 2-25, by using edit mode.

Figure 2-25. *Closer look at Stroke object in edit mode*

As you can see in Figure 2-25, the line that is in the black strokes are the points, well, not vertices since this is not yet a mesh, and these points help to modify the strokes. See an example of it in Figure 2-26.

Figure 2-26. *Modifying Monkey object*

As you can see in Figure 2-26, I modify the monkey object using the transform tool. I just modify its eyebrow by moving and rotating it, and the same with its mouth. Also, I transform its mouth and eyes by scaling them. But the most important thing is that I'm able to transform it by selecting the points. You cannot transform parts without the points like the forehead in the monkey. Okay, for a better explanation, take a look at Figure 2-27.

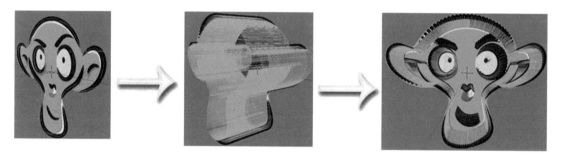

Figure 2-27. *Extruding Monkey object*

As you can see in Figure 2-27, the ones that have been extruded are those in the sides because they were the ones with the points. The one in the middle, or the orange one, are a fill color for monkey that can be found in the object data panel under the properties section.

Okay. Let's now proceed to the next object, which is the armature.

Armature Object

Armatures are for characters. You used it for posing and of course for creating animation. These objects have three modes: object mode, edit mode, and pose mode. Take a look at Figure 2-28 to see how this object looks.

Figure 2-28. *Armature object*

You can only use this object for making poses animation. Games have characters. If you want to create your character and be the one to rig it, or have the bones for its animation, you can learn more about this armature object. Its tools lie mostly in pose mode and in the object Data panel under properties. It has a few tools in edit mode like extruding the bone.

Take a look at Figure 2-29 to see some basic modifications for the armature.

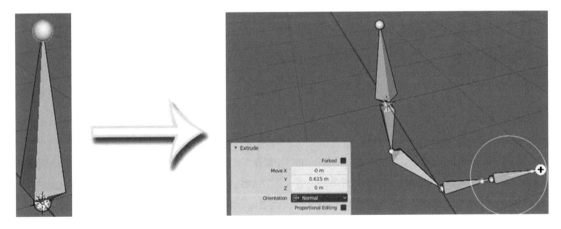

Figure 2-29. *Basic modification for Armature object*

As you can see, I just simply use extrude and the minimum of the rotate tool for modifying the armature or the bones. And yes, its shape is just like that.

Let's now proceed to the next object, which is the lattice.

Lattice Object

Lattice objects only have object mode and edit mode. They have only basic editing tools. Then, what is the use of this object?

Lattice consists of a three-dimensional non-renderable grid of vertices, and its main use is to apply a deformation to the object it controls with a lattice modifier. The lattice should be scaled and moved to fit around your object in object mode. Take a look at Figure 2-30 to see how the lattice object looks and how it works.

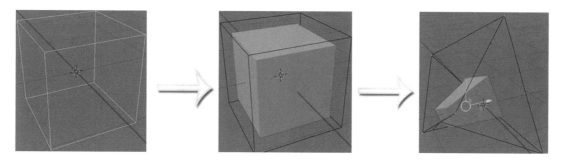

Figure 2-30. *Lattice and how it works*

There aren't many available tools for editing or modifying lattice objects. Okay. You may ask, if this is for editing an existing object such as meshes, curves, surfaces, texts, and particles, why not just directly edit or modify those objects in edit mode instead of using the lattice? Well, here's a reason you will consider using this. If your mesh object already has many vertices, it will be hard for you to modify it, especially if you only want to modify just a part of it. So here is the lattice to help you just select the part of that mesh and modify it smoothly. It can also allow you to edit multiple objects in a scene since objects are allowed to use the same lattice. It's just like a container.

So now, let's proceed to the next object, which is the empty object.

Empty Objects

Empties. Literally empty objects but they have a purpose. They might have no volume and surfaces, and just a single coordinate point with no geometry, but they have their own uses. Depending on the empty object characteristics, they have their own purposes. Some of them are useful for animation while some are useful for reference.

Empties can serve as transform handles too. They can also be parented to other objects, which gives you the ability to control a group of objects easily. They can be used as a target for constraints like bone. Lastly, they can also be used in an array modifier to help you move only one object by using this as the offset and to other modifiers like mirror, wave, displace, etc.

Don't forget: since they don't have volume or surfaces to edit on, they only have the object mode.

Take a look at Figure 2-31 to see the list of empty objects.

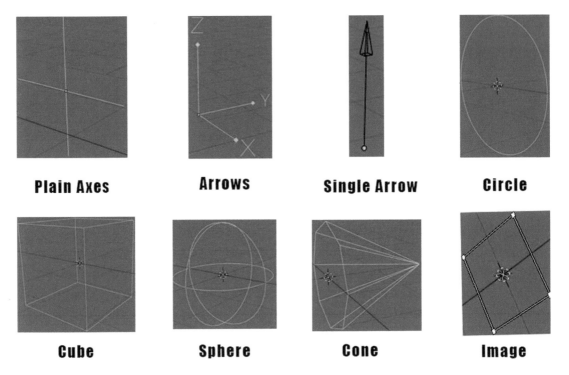

Figure 2-31. *List of Empty Objects*

So, how do each of these empty objects work? Let's take a look in Figures 2-32 and 2-33 to see how empty objects work.

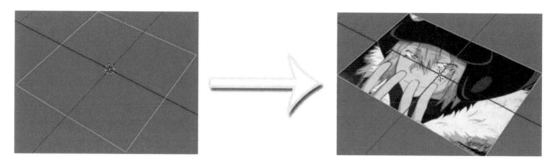

Figure 2-32. *Image Empty Object works*

I add the image by first adding an empty image, then going to the **Object Data panel** in **Properties ➤ Image ➤ Open**.

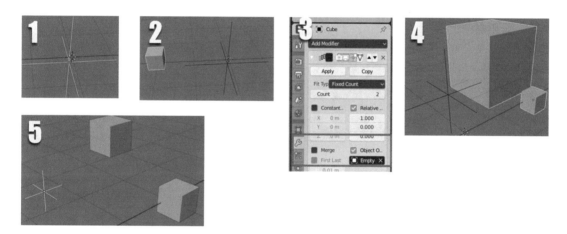

Figure 2-33. *Plain Axes Empty works*

I used an array modifier for this example. I add the array modifier in the cube, then set it to empty in the object offset as you can see in number 3. As you can see in our example, in numbers 4 and 5, the plain axes affect the size of the added cube from the array modifier. As I scale the plain axes, the cube also scales down.

Plain axes, arrows, single arrows, circles, cubes, spheres, and cones are all empties that can be used in arrays, constraints, animations, and objects parenting. Their only difference is the effect on the base on their structure or how it can help you make your project easier than the other one. For example, the arrows can help you create a 360-degree camera effect easily by parenting an object to it, then animating the empty itself.

Note that you can drag and drop images into the scene to get these references into Blender.

There is another object next to empty, which is image, but it acts exactly like image empty so I will skip it and go to the next one, light objects.

Light and Light Probe Objects

As its name suggest, light objects give light to the scene. On one hand, we only have object mode for this type of object, and you can only edit some basic data from it through the object data panel in the properties, though you can do some scaling, moving, and rotating too. Light probes, on the other hand, record lighting information locally to light the scene using indirect lighting. Eevee used them as support objects.

Take a look at Figure 2-34 to see the list of light objects to see how they work.

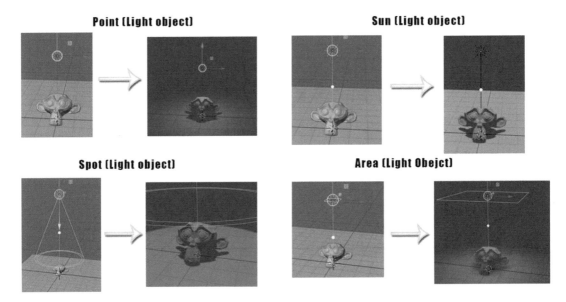

Figure 2-34. *List of Light objects and how they work*

You can see in Figure 2-34 how these light objects differ from each other by their effects. Not only that, they also differ when it comes to the strength of their light. For example, if you gave a sun light 10 watts (you can do this in **Properties ➤ Object Data Panel ➤ under Sun ➤ Strength**), the output is too bright; but if you gave that value of strength to area, you will not see its effect – just like our example in Figure 2-35.

Area (Light Object)   **Sun (Light Object)**

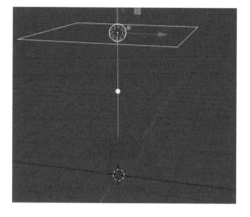

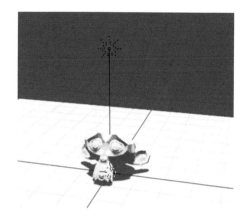

Figure 2-35. *Area Light vs. Sun Light*

This is because the sun lamp has a multiplier to account for the distance of the actual sun from the Earth and since the lighting system, especially in cycles, is physically accurate, you'd have to set the sun lamp to more than 1,000,000 and place it hundreds of thousands of miles away in the 3D world for it to be accurate.

Now let's take a look at Figure 2-36 to see a list of light probe objects.

Reflection Cubemap

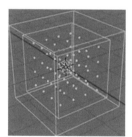

Irradiance Volume

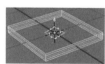

Reflection Plane

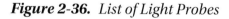

Figure 2-36. *List of Light Probes*

Light probes are made for Eevee engines and more for photorealistic rendering. Reflection planes are for flat surfaces like mirrors. They calculate reflection maps for reflective surfaces. Reflection cubemap is similar to reflection plane but for curving shapes like sphere and cubes. Though Eevee already has screen space reflection to do the task, these objects can help in some case scenarios since screen space reflections have its limits too. Irradiance volume acts differently. It calculates indirect lighting and shadows rather than reflection.

Take a look at Figure 2-37 to see how reflection cubemap works.

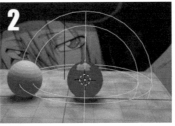

Figure 2-37. *Reflection Cubemap at work*

First stop, I make the material for the sphere a glass or a reflective one by setting its roughness to 0, transmission to 1, and changing its color to white in the material panel in properties. You can also do this in the node editor. Next, I select the sphere by holding **Shift + S**, so the shortcut for selection for the snapping will appear, and choose **Cursor to Selected**. Then, I add the reflection cubemap by pressing **Shift + A,** then go to **Light Probe ➤ Reflection Cubemap**. The result will not appear right away. You need to bake the cubemap by going to **Render Properties Panel in Properties Editor ➤ Indirect Lightning ➤ Bake Cubemap only** as you can see in Figure 2-38.

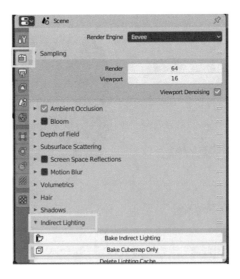

Figure 2-38. *Render Panel ➤ Indirect Lighting ➤ Bake Cubemap Only*

Take a look at Figure 2-39 to see how the reflection plane works.

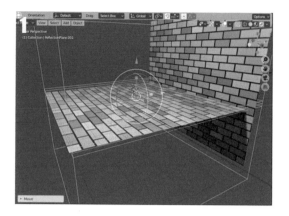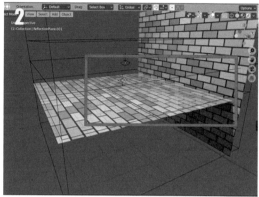

Figure 2-39. *Reflection Plane at work*

Its process is the same as reflection cubemap. You need to bake it in the indirect light section in the render properties panel at the properties editor to make it work, but there's a little difference. If in the reflection cubemap, you will turn the color of your mesh to white, here you will darken the color of your mesh to make it look like a mirror. Since the concept of a mirror is a transparent glass covered by something darker at its other side, you will make your mesh color darker. Even though I already baked my reflection plane, nothing appears on the first picture. In order for me to be able to see the effect, I need to adjust its scope by adjusting the value of its distance in **Properties ➤ Object Data ➤ Probe ➤ Distance** as you can see in Figure 2-40.

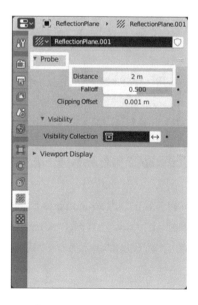

Figure 2-40. *Object Data Panel ➤ Probe ➤ Distance*

Before we proceed to the next object, let's see how the irradiance volume works in Figure 2-41.

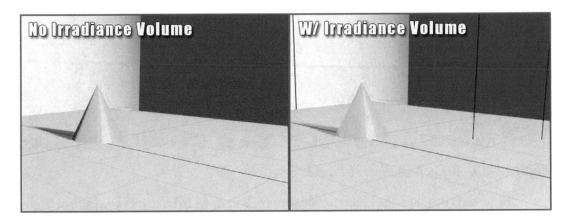

Figure 2-41. *Irradiance Volume at work*

In this example, I used a spotlight to be the source light with 50,000 watts. You can see in Figure 2-41 that irradiance volume gives a softer look at your scene compared to the one without irradiance volume. You can notice the changes, especially in the shadow, and how brighter the scene becomes. It calculates all of the light paths and the reason it looks softer and brighter is that it takes bounce lighting into account, which Eevee doesn't naturally do.

I'd like to note that this is for Eevee engine only!

Now, let's proceed to our next objects, which are the camera and speaker.

Camera and Speaker Objects

Camera is for capturing the scene you created for rendering purposes. For modeling, you can take it also as an object to help you see if your objects are in their right place. For animation, of course it has a vital role. You cannot create an animation (just like a film or movie) without a camera.

Speaker is for audio, obviously. It provides sounds in the 3D viewport.

Both the camera and speaker only have an object mode. Camera, by default, has already been set once you open your Blender or a new Blend file.

Figure 2-42 shows how these look.

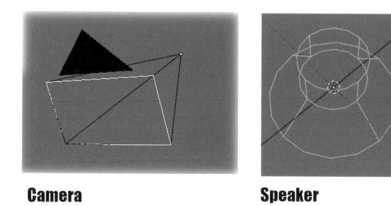

Figure 2-42. *Camera and Speaker*

What's left now are the objects related to **Force Field Objects,** which are Force, Wind, Vortex, Magnetic, Harmonic, Charge, Lennard-Jones, Texture, Curve Guide, Boid, Turbulence, Drag, and Smoke Flow, but I decided not to discuss much of it since they are more for animations and simulations, and it takes more pages to discuss these objects effectively.

Now, we're already done in our introduction and we'll proceed to our main dish, which is about the modeling tools, which can be found in modeling workspace; and features of Blender that can help you create a game asset or game environment. I'll be discussing this along with a sample project so it will be more fun for everyone. After all, examples are great ways of teaching.

Modeling Specific Tools

Blenders have tools that you can use even you're doing things like sculpting, texturing, UV mapping, or just simply layout. There are also tools that are specific in those things. In this part, we'll be focusing more on the specific modeling tools for modeling.

Take a look at Figure 2-43 to see the toolbar for modeling workspace, which you can also see in edit mode.

Figure 2-43. *Toolbar for Modeling workspace (General: Red; Modeling Specific: Yellow)*

The toolbar for modeling workspace has six general tools (I just called it general tools) and twelve modeling specific tools, based on icons present. Yes, there are more tools in it. As you can see in Figure 2-43, there are small triangles beside the icons of some tools. This means there are other tools hidden in it. So, let's now start discussing these modeling tools.

Extrude Region

Extrude region tool, which you can use by holding shift + spacebar + E in your keyboard, is used to extrude freely in any axis, whether there are vertices, edges, or faces. Take a look at Figure 2-44 to see it works.

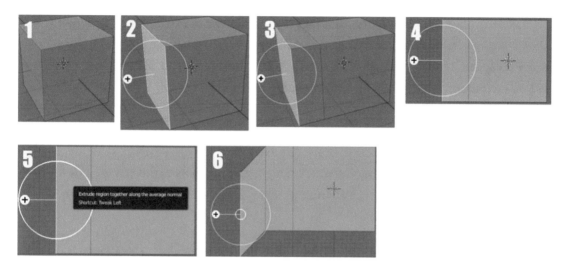

Figure 2-44. *Extrude Region at work*

There are two things that I'd like to point out in this tool: the plus and the white circle around the plus. Okay. Let's start with the white circle. When you select something to extrude, like, as for our example, the face, the plus and the white circle will automatically appear as an indicator that you can already extrude that part. When you place your cursor in the white circle, you will extrude in a different axis where the plus sign is facing just like you can see in Figure 2-44 in numbers 5 and 6. It changes the direction of your extruding. Now, let's talk about the plus. When you click and drag using the plus mark, you will extrude that part in the axis where it was pointing. If you wonder what is the basis of the plus mark, it follows the facing of the normals of your objects. Take a look at Figure 2-45 for you to know how to enable seeing the normals of your objects and to see how it works together with the extrude tool.

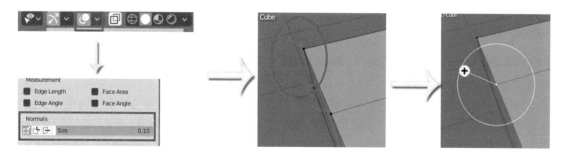

Figure 2-45. *Enabling Normals*

Let's now discuss the tool that you can see together with extrude region. When you click the triangle, you will see a drop-down menu with a list of four tools including the extrude region. The other three are extrude along normals, extrude individual, and extrude to cursor. Let's start with extrude along normals.

Extrude Along Normals

This tool will only extrude along the axis facing by the normals of the selected part to be extruded. Unlike the extrude region, there is no option of being redirected. Take a look at Figure 2-46 to see how it works.

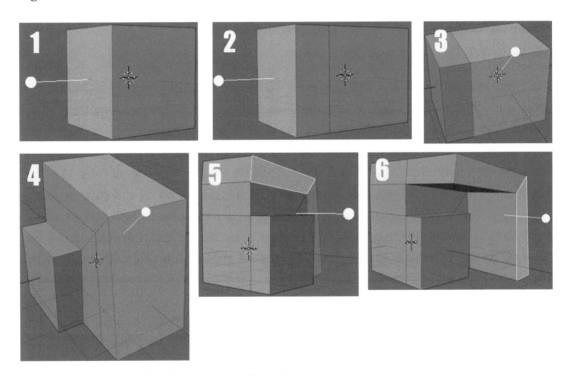

Figure 2-46. *Extrude Along Normals tool at work*

You can see in images 3, 4, 5, and 6 that after I select the two faces, they extrude together. You can also notice that the arrow in image 4 looks like it is in the center. This is because in extrude along normals, its computation for extruding is based on the selected elements' local normals. You will understand this more after discussing the next tool, which is the extrude individual where the output is opposite to this tool. This tool has a shortcut key of Shift + Spacebar + 9.

Note that if you press Shift+ Spacebar + 9 all in a quick succession, it will actually enable the tool push and pull, but if you press Shift + Spacebar and then pause for the menu and press 9, it will take you to extrude along normals.

Extrude Individual

As I said above, its output is opposite of the extrude along normals. It extrudes each individual face along its normal. Yes, only for faces. Not for vertices, not for edges. And this can also access by holding Shift + Spacebar + 0. Take a look at Figure 2-47 to see how this tool works.

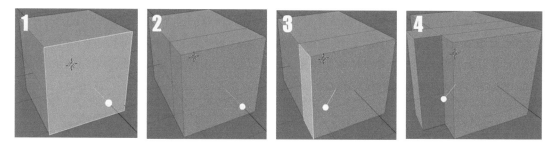

Figure 2-47. *Extrude Individual tool at work*

As you can see, at first, if you only select one face, it looks similar with extrude along normals; but if you select more than one, that's the time you can see its difference. This is because, as its name suggested, it extrudes individually.

Extrude to Cursor

This tool extrudes vertices, edges, or even faces toward where your cursor is or where you click your cursor. Take a look at Figure 2-48 to see how it works.

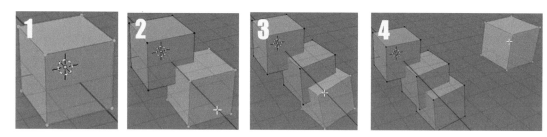

Figure 2-48. *Extrude Individual tool at work*

You notice that the duplicate or extruded part is located at the place where your cursor is. Okay. I guess this can be used if you want to create a small object with some base mesh, but you don't want to use the particle system and you just want to randomly spread it in the scene. That's what I'm actually thinking when I want to give an example on how this tool works. You can use it, too, for getting rough forms for modeling and sculpting, like for body shapes or hair. You can select a group of faces and then just click away, and it can help get organic shapes using some scaling and grabbing or rotovating. Also, this tool is one of the few tools that doesn't have settings.

Inset Faces

This tool inserts new faces to selected faces. For this tool, even you are able to select edges, unless it doesn't form a face, it will not work. For example, if you just select three edges, this will not work since four edges are equivalent to one face. Okay, take a look at Figure 2-49 to see how this tool works.

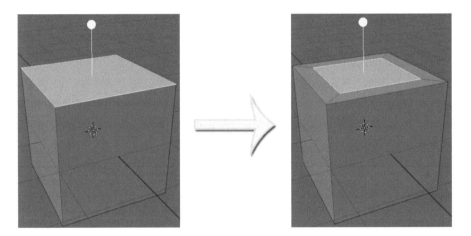

Figure 2-49. *Inset Face tool at work*

In order to achieve this kind of output, after you select the place you want to have your new face inserted, you need to first click the yellow arrow, or press I in the keyboard, and drag it to the center.

Bevel

This tool cuts the edges to create a bevel effect to your objects. Unlike inset, this works with vertices, edges, and faces. Take a look at Figure 2-50 to see how it works.

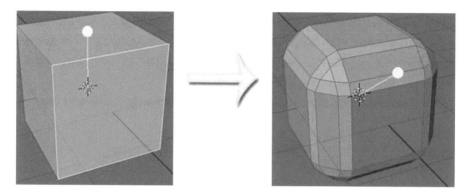

Figure 2-50. *Bevel tool at work*

This tool helps smooth the edges of your object, which is necessary for a realistic look since we all know is that there is no perfect cube or rectangle in real life.

Loop Cut

This tool cuts the mesh with a loop. You can also slide the loop before you make the cut. Take a look at Figure 2-51 to see how it works.

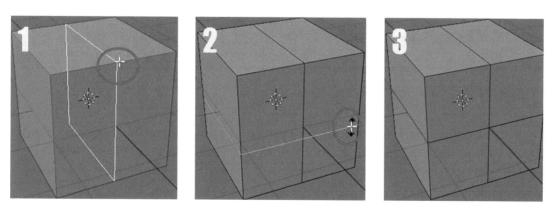

Figure 2-51. *Loop cut tool at work*

Once you choose the loop cut tool, whenever you position your cursor in the mesh, the loop will already position itself where your cursor is, just like in image 1. Just like in image 2, when you want to slide the loop before you make the cut, you need to drag it by holding the left mouse button. Note that when you drag the loop, it will only be dragged between the two cuts where it was located so before you slide the loop, make sure you already positioned it in the place where you wanted it to be placed. Also, as you can see in image 2, when you slide the loop, you will see a black arrow with two heads facing both sides. This indicates that the loop is being dragged, and also this arrow shows which direction the loop can slide on.

Just like extrude, there is another tool that can be seen together with loop cut. It is the offset edge loop cut.

Offset Edge Loop Cut

This tool is dependent. Yes. Dependent with loop cut. It will not work without a loop cut. As its name suggested, it offsets the edge loop slide. What it does is when you already have a loop cut, it will create a loop cut from a loop cut. Not that clear? Okay. Here's a visual representation. Take a look at Figure 2-52.

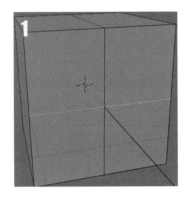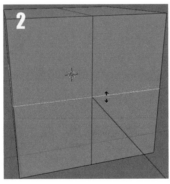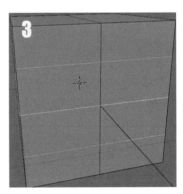

Figure 2-52. *Offset Edge Loop cut tool at work*

Based on Figure 2-52, we can say that these tools make the loop cutting easier. Since as I mentioned earlier, in loop cut, when you already choose to slide a loop, it will only slide in between two cuts. So, if you want to have a cut in the opposite side, you need to make another loop. As you can see here, in images 2 and 3, when we already drag the loop from the center, it creates two loop, where one is one going to the top side and one to the bottom side. And because these two loops are dragged together, at the same time, they are the same sizes.

Knife Tool

Of course, the knife tool is used to cut mesh. You can say it is applicable if you want to add vertices or edges randomly or the way you just wanted to. Take a look at Figure 2-53 to see how it works in actual use.

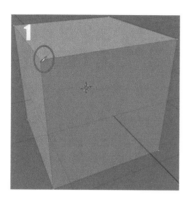
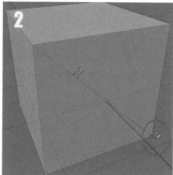
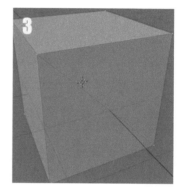

Figure 2-53. *Knife tool at work*

When you activate the knife tool, your cursor will turn into a knife, just like in image 1. When you start slicing your mesh, unless you press enter, just like you can see in image 2, the slicing will not stop.

Bisect Tool

Together with the knife tool is the bisect tool. For this tool, you need either edges or faces to be selected. Yes, this is not applicable if you only have like one vertex selected. Take a look at Figure 2-54 to see how it works.

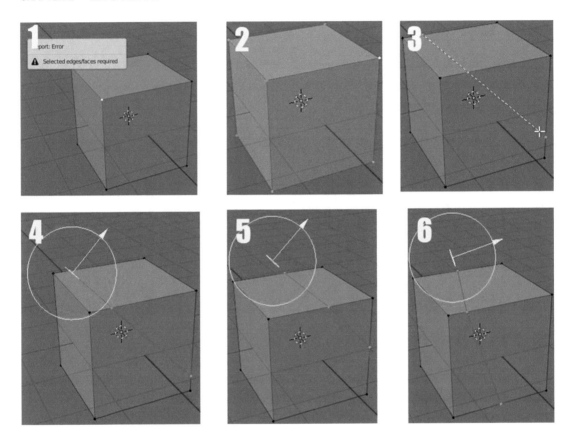

Figure 2-54. *Bisect tool at work*

Image 1 in Figure 2-54 shows the error you will encounter when you just select one vertex and use the bisect tool. When you use this tool, first you will select the part where you want to bisect and then select the portion or part by holding and dragging your cursor just like you can see in image 3. You can notice from images 4–6 that there is this yellow arrow and a blue circle around it. The yellow arrow helps you slide the loops or edges created by the bisect tool, and the circle helps you change the position by rotating it.

Poly Build Tool

In version 2.80, you just need to click and create three to four vertices, and then press the F key to create a face using Poly Build tool. In version 2.82, which I'm currently using for this book, what we have for this tool is that you need to at least have a mesh object, and the easiest one is a plane, then click one edge of it and drag it out. After you drag it out, it will form a new face. But wait, there is also an indicator when you can drag it out and form a new face. Take a look at Figure 2-55 to see how the new setup for the Poly build tool works.

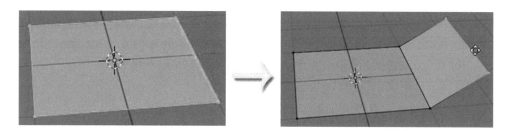

Figure 2-55. *Poly build tool at work*

The blue color in the edge that you can see in Figure 2-55 indicates that you can already drag it and create a new face. I'd like to note that this tool is more for retopology.

Spin Tool

This tool extrudes selected vertices in a circle around the cursor indicated in the viewport. To use this tool, you must at least have an existing vertex or vertices that it can extrude. Take a look at Figure 2-56 to see how it works.

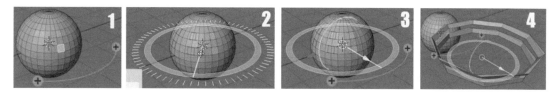

Figure 2-56. *Spin tool at work*

The blue curve with the plus sign at the endpoint of it is used to spin your selected elements. What you can see in image 2, the gray circle that surrounds the sphere, indicates the spinning you are currently doing. After you've done the extruding and spinning, two arrows will show: a green one; and a red one, which you can use to move the extruded part created by the spin tool. The red arrow is for the X-axis and the green arrow, of course, is for the Y-axis.

Spin Duplicates

Spin duplicates is the same as with Spin tool. It also have a blue curve that you use for spinning and a gray circle that when you do the spinning, shows the green and red arrows after you've done extruding and spinning, and it also has the same output. So, what makes it different? It duplicates the data of the main objects or elements. There is no figure for this one since the output will be the same as the spin tool.

Smooth Tool and Randomize Tool

The smooth tool flattens angles of the selected vertices. You can see a yellow arrow to selected elements when you use it. You can say this is more useful when you already have many vertices and you want to make your object smoother.

The randomize tool, as its name suggests, randomly arranges selected vertices. Just like the smooth tool, it also has the yellow arrow to a selected element when you use it.

Take a look at Figure 2-57 to see how these two tools work.

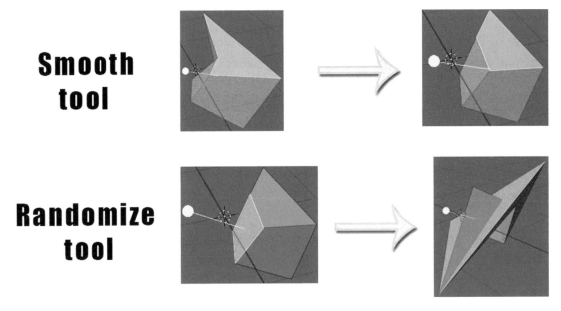

Figure 2-57. *Smooth and Randomize tools at work*

You can see in Figure 2-57 how the smooth tool changes the mesh object from having rough edges to a mesh object with smooth edges. With the randomize tool, you can see how it randomly scaled out the face selected.

Edge Slide Tool and Vertex Slide Tool

The edge slide and vertex slide have the same function and settings. The difference is that the edge slide, as its name suggests, affects the edge; while the vertex slide affects the vertex. So let's take a look at Figure 2-58 to see how these two tools work.

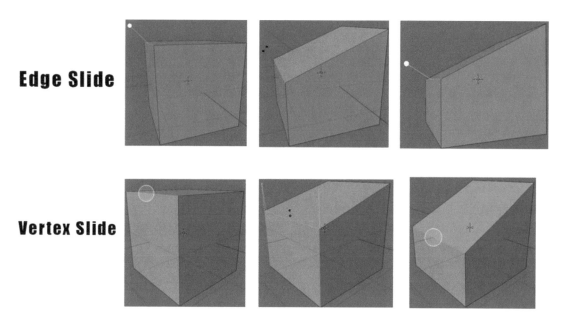

Figure 2-58. *Edge Slide and Vertex Slide tools at work*

As you can see in Figure 2-58, they have the same output and same function, but as you can clearly see, even though I selected an edge to slide for the vertex slide tool, it shows how it affects the vertex by showing the previous position of the vertices that have been dragged.

Shrink/Flatten Tool

This tool simply shrinks or flattens the elements along the direction of the normal. It is like the transform tool, which is part of the general tool, since when you select just a face and apply it, it looks like you're just moving the face; but when you select the whole mesh, it appears like you are scaling the whole mesh. The transform tool can scale, move, and rotate an object. In my opinion, the difference between the transform tool and the shrink/flatten tool, aside from shrinking/flattening can't rotate any elements; it is specific to modeling unlike the other one. However, the transform tool can be used in other workspaces. Another difference between the shrink/flatten tool and transform tool is its settings. It has a proportional falloff option and offset.

Push/Pull Tool

If the shrink/flatten tool is like the move tool, the push/pull tool is like the scale tool. It pushes or pulls the selected elements. It also has the same settings as the shrink/flatten tool.

Take a look at Figure 2-59 to see how the shrink/flatten tool and the push/pull tool work.

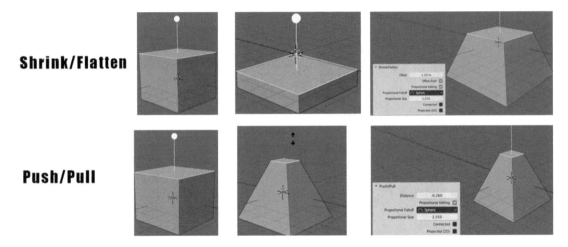

Figure 2-59. *Shrink/Flatten and Push/Pull tool at work*

As you can see in Figure 2-59, both the shrink/flatten and push/pull tools have a yellow arrow with a round head. This arrow indicates where your Normal is pointing. The settings will not appear unless you already dragged the selected item. Just like in our example, you cannot see the settings when I click the face. But after the application, when I have flattened the cube for shrink/flatten and scaled in for push/pull, its settings appear. That's only the time you can play with the proportional falloff – if you enable proportional editing and other settings they have.

Shear Tool

Now we have a shear tool. This tool shears selected items along the horizontal axis of the screen.

When you select the shear tool, there are arrows pointing to different axes appearing on the selected elements to modify. When you click and drag the head of this arrow, which looks like the letter X, the selected element is sheared to the axis, toward the Y-axis, or even in the Z-axis; it depends on which direction the X arrow head is pointing to. You can also change the direction by changing the offset value and axis in its settings

Take a look at Figure 2-60 to see how this tool works.

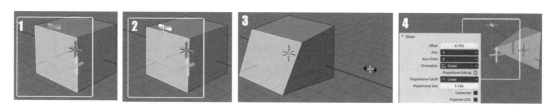

Figure 2-60. *Shear tool at work*

As you can see in Figure 2-60, we have three arrows connected to each other, and the arrow head looks like the letter X. Each arrow head represents two axes. The arrow with the yellow-orange head represents the X-Y-axis; the arrow with the pink-violet arrow head represents the X-Z-axis; and the arrow with the green-blue arrow head represents the Y-Z-axis.

To Sphere Tool

Let's talk about the to sphere. This tool moves the selected vertices outward in a spherical shape around the mesh center.

Take a look at Figure 2-61 to see how the to sphere tool works.

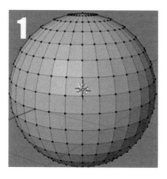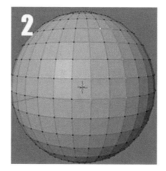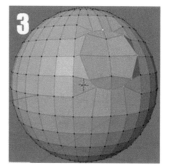

Figure 2-61. *To Sphere tool at work*

As you can see in Figure 2-61, after I dragged out the selected vertices, it formed a spherical shape. You cannot appreciate its function if you only selected three vertices in line with each other, or two faces in line with each other. Since it forms a spherical shape, it is best when you select vertices, edges, or faces that you will make in a form of a circle.

Rip Region Tool and Rip Edge Tool

The rip region is only applicable with vertices while the rip edge tool is applicable to both vertices and edges. When you use rip edge in faces, you cannot see its effect. It only moves the face. Rip regions rip polygons while the rip edge rips the vertices. Also, rip region extends the vertices and automatically connects them to other vertices while rip edge extends the edge and cuts or rips it out from the mesh.

Take a look at Figure 2-62 to see how these tools work.

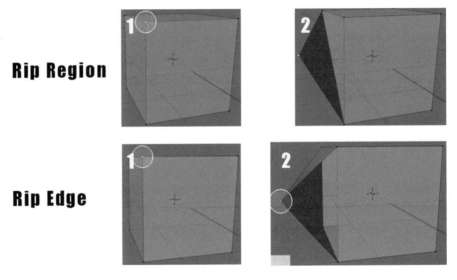

Figure 2-62. *Rip Region and Rip Edge tools at work*

Now, we're going to proceed to the last part of this chapter: a sample project with a discussion. For this one, we'll go for creating a game asset for a game environment rather than a whole game environment so we can at least discuss more with fewer pages. After all, you cannot create a game environment without the game asset.

So, now, let's start the fun!

Sample Project - Pawn Chess Piece

Yes, we'll be doing a chess piece here as a sample project. The first step, of course, is that we need a reference. I'd like to note here that in making a game environment, or even just a game asset, it is still important that you have a story or a theme for it. If you don't have, trust me – you will get lost. What I mean is, if you are like me who can easily be filled with ideas, then you will be confused as to what you will do and end up doing nothing. So, it is better that you have your theme or story as a basis for the game assets you will be creating. Don't worry. You don't need to become a novel writer to come up with a story. You just need your imagination. Imagine what makes you happy or excited. If that doesn't work, take a look at what kind of movies/dramas/comic books/stories you are fond of. You can get ideas from them. Just take a look around you.

For this step, Figures 2-63 to 2-75 will be about modeling the pawn piece. So, first, we need a reference image. I searched my reference image in Google, though there are other sites where you can search too, like Pinterest, Flickr, 500px, etc. I check for both the front view and the top view for this model.

Let's now start the modeling.

First, I'll import my reference image in Blender by pressing Shift + A then going to Image ➤ Reference. You can also just drag and drop images into the 3D viewport, in the background, if you are in object mode. You can also do this by going to Add menu ➤ Image ➤ Reference. I'd like to note that for you to effectively use this reference image object, you must already be in the axis or view where you wanted to use your reference image. For example, I want to use my reference image in the right view side, so I will set my 3D viewport view to the right view by pressing numpad 3 or going to View menu ➤ Viewpoint ➤ Right.

Ok. Let's take a look at Figure 2-64.

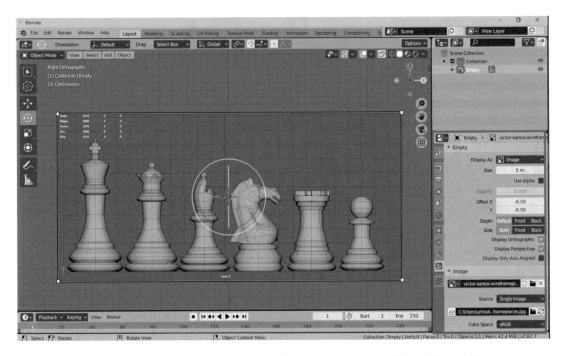

Figure 2-63. *Image Reference Object. Reference Image credit to Victor Santos: (www.artstation.com/artwork/qAJV92)*

The one in the red rectangle is the properties panel. Since what we currently have is the image reference object, what you can see in the object data are the settings or details pertaining to the reference image object.

First, I'd like to note that it is recommended that you reduce your vertices to lower the value as much as possible so you can work with your game assets with ease. You can reduce the vertices of any meshes by changing their settings when it pops up after you add your mesh, just like you can see in Figure 2-64.

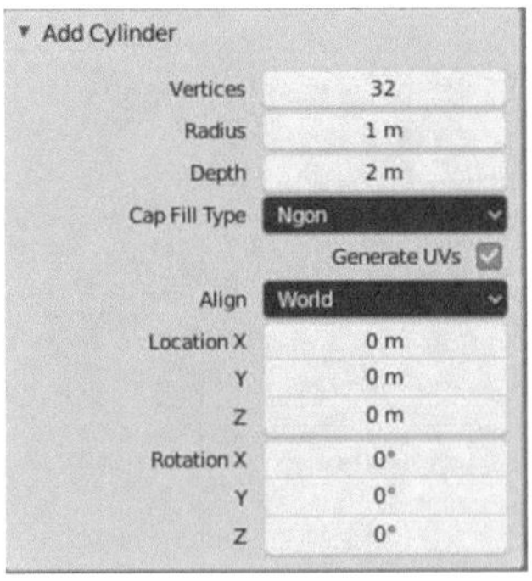

Figure 2-64. *Settings for changing vertices*

By lowering the value of vertices, for example, take 32, divide by 2, and this will be 16, so you can have a lower number vertices that can help you with your work.

Since we we're going to use our reference image object for modeling, we lower the opacity of the image so we can see our model while our image is at the back of it. But as you can see in Figure 2-65, the opacity is disabled. It was because the "Use Alpha" setting is unchecked. So, I will toggle it up so I can enable opacity.

Now, we'll start modeling our pawn by adding a cylinder. Again, I add a cylinder by holding Shift + A ➤ Mesh ➤ Cylinder. You can also do this by going to Add menu ➤ Mesh ➤ Cylinder. At this moment, I'm still using the layout workspace so I can create the pawn object as a separate object. You can also do this in the modeling workspace by just changing the mode type into an object mode.

I just set the opacity of the image reference to 0.392 so I can trace my model to the image effectively. I'd like to note that for you to avoid having a hard time later, make sure that you will not deform your base mesh. Just like in this pawn, if I ever deform the cylinder because I'm scaling it up to fit in the reference image, which usually happens to beginners, it will become harder later for to create a smooth look for the pawn piece. Just remember, we don't need to be too detailed at first. We just need to see the shape that resembles our reference image. For our pawn, we have a cylinder. We just need to place the cylinder next to the reference image just like what you can see in Figure 2-65.

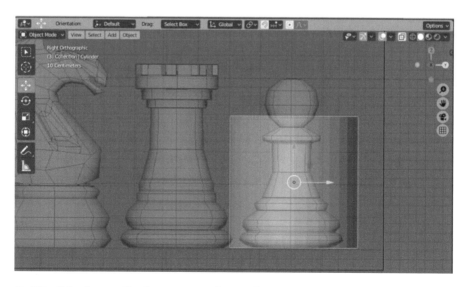

Figure 2-65. *Placing cylinder next to the Reference Image*

I didn't scale it up since I will also do it later on as we model it to be like the pawn. But for now, let's start the first phase of modeling.

Switching to modeling workspace (or from object mode to edit mode), you can see that the whole cylinder is highlighted, meaning the whole cylinder is selected. Just click outside and it will be deselected. By default, your selection is set to vertices. You can change it to edges or faces in the settings next to the type mode select menu, as you can see in Figure 2-66; but for this example, we will use vertices to select those we will edit.

Figure 2-66. *Red Rectangle: selection settings for vertices, edges, and faces*

I also change my view, in 3D viewport, from solid to wireframe view by pressing Z on the keyboard and then clicking wireframe. You can also do it by going to the shading setting, which is located in the top-right view of your 3D view port, just like what you see in Figure 2-67. In solid view, you can see the actual design of your object, but in wireframe, you can see the edges and vertices like it was an x-ray view of your object. It is easier to manage your vertices in this way.

Figure 2-67. *Red Rectangle: Shading settings*

From the left side will be the Wireframe, Solid, Material Preview, and Rendered.

Next, I'll start the transforming by selecting the vertices at the bottom of the cylinder by pressing B (or the Select Box tool). Then scale it to fit on the reference image as you can see in Figure 2-68.

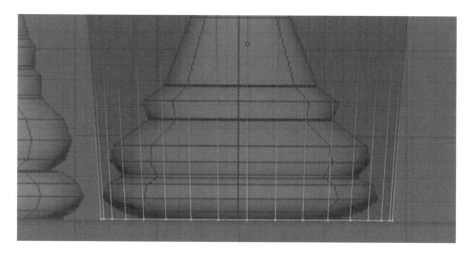

Figure 2-68. *Scaling the selected vertices at the bottom*

Then, I press Ctrl + R to add a loop to the cylinder so I can add a shape that is at least similar to the reference image you see in Figure 2-69.

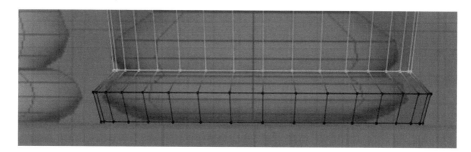

Figure 2-69. *Adding new loop*

At this point, the only thing I'll do is to add a loop and move the loop by pressing G. But of course, I make that sure before I move the loop, all vertices are selected.

I'd like to note that when you use Ctrl + R when adding the loop, until you press enter, the loop you are adding will not be applied. Also, before you press enter, it's better if you go ahead and choose the right location for your loop so you don't need to move it too much.

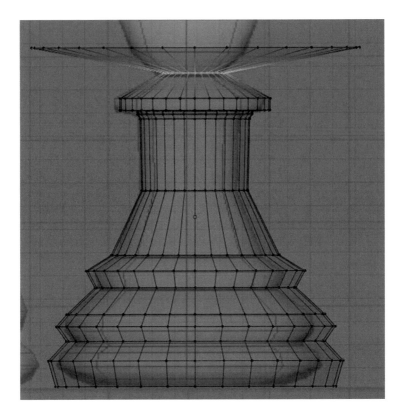

Figure 2-70. *Current progress of the Pawn*

Now, as you can see in Figure 2-70, we already covered the body of the pawn, but the head is still not yet done and we already used the base mesh. This is the time now where extruding will be handy. First, I'll scale the last loop to fit to the lower part of the head of the pawn and then start extruding by pressing E on the keyboard. You can also use the extrude region tool for this.

What I'm going to do here for the head is just extruding and scaling.

Now, let's see in Figure 2-71 the current progress of our pawn.

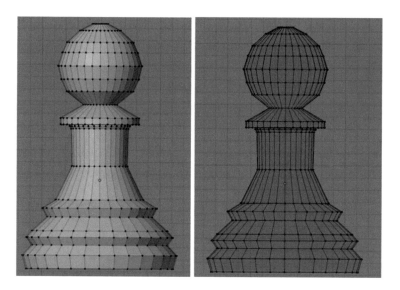

Figure 2-71. *Current progress of the Pawn (Left: Solid mode, Right: Wireframe)*

As you can see in Figure 2-71, it already takes shape: from just a simple cylinder to a pawn chess piece. Now, let's smooth it by using a modifier called subdivision surface.

Subdivision surface is a modifier used to split faces of mesh into smaller ones, making a smooth look on mesh. It helps you to lessen the usage of too many vertices just to smooth out your mesh.

Figure 2-72. *Subdivision surface Modifier Settings*

You can see in Figure 2-72 the settings of the subdivision surface modifier. **Render** indicates the number of subdivisions that will be performed when rendering; **viewport** indicates the number of subdivisions that will be performed in the 3D viewport; **quality** is how precisely the vertices are positioned; **Catmull-Clark** is the default option and subdivides plus smoothes the surfaces while **simple** only subdivides the surfaces.

The other options with a select menu in the settings of the subdivision surface is for handling the UVs during the subdivision. It has two options that are **smooth, keep corners** wherein the UV islands are smoothed but the boundaries are sharp and the **sharp** wherein the UVs are unchanged.

Take a look at Figure 2-73 to see the effect of subdivision surface (or subsurface) to our model.

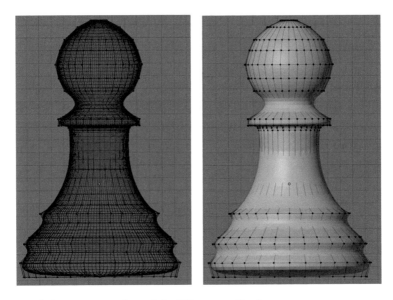

Figure 2-73. *Subdivision surface Modifier applied*

See how smooth our pawn was. Now, let's adjust our vertices to fit into our interests: just a basic commands now like G for move and/or S for scale. Note that you need to switch back to solid mode in order to see the image on the right.

If you continue to do this project, you might notice the ugly part at the bottom of the pawn just like what you can see in Figure 2-74.

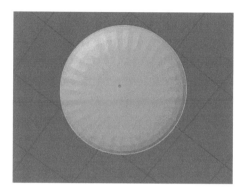

Figure 2-74. *Bottom of the Pawn*

The reason for this is because we are using geometry. Remember that base mesh is a cylinder, and then we add a subsurface modifier. You can say that the face at the bottom of the cylinder mesh becomes too crowded because of too many vertices that it already can't handle. So, in order to fix this, first, we need to select the vertices or faces involved, and then we're going to use the inset tool by pressing I, then dragging it inward. By doing this, it seems that you are adding another loop and it smooths that part of your mesh. Last, after I have done the editing, I make it smoother by going to Object Menu ➤ Shade Smooth.

Now we already have our final model for a pawn chess piece as you can see in Figure 2-75.

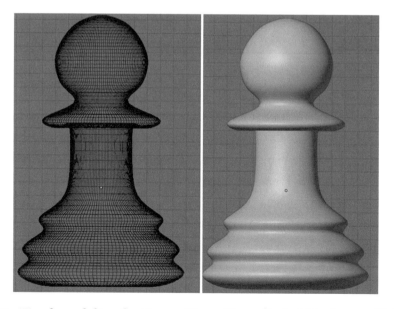

Figure 2-75. *Final modeling for Pawn Chess Piece (Left: Wireframe, Right: Solid)*

Sample Project - Rook Chess Piece

I'll start now with the next chess piece, which is the rook. With the same process, I'll add a cylinder and place it next to the reference image. Then I'll make a first phase of modeling by scaling and moving the vertices in the wireframe view.

Let's take a look at Figure 2-76 to catch a glimpse of the process of how I did this rook piece.

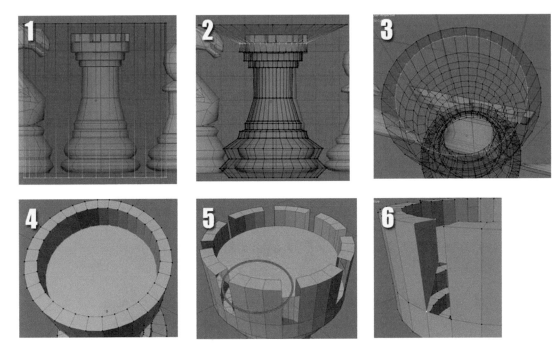

Figure 2-76. *First Phase of Rook piece*

In image 1, you can see how I place the cylinder next to the reference image. In image 2, you can see how I scale and move the vertices so I can fit it to the image reference. In image 3, you can see how I use the inset tool to create a loop cut at the top of the cylinder base mesh to create the top part of the rook piece. For me to achieve the result in image 4, what I did is while the loop cut, I recently made using the inset tool was selected, you can press G for move then Y for Y axis to restrain the movement to Y axis. If you want to scale only in Y-axis, press S for scale then Y key. If you want to rotate in Y axis only, press R for rotate then Y key. If you want to restrict the movement in Z-axis, you can press G for move, then Z for Z-axis. To limit the scaling in Z axis, just press S for scaling key then Z key. And to limit the rotation to Z-axis, press R for rotation then Z key.

Let's now proceed to image 5 of Figure 2-76. For reference, let's call the one inside the red oblong, in Figure 2-76 image 5, a column. In order for me to achieve the output that you can see in image 5, I divided the 32 columns by 8. So, we have 4 columns in each group. Then I delete one column in each group. In this way, I get an even number of columns in each group. Since we delete this, we called it a column, which is composed of vertices and faces, and we create a hole in our mesh. Just like you can see in image 6, in order to fix this, I select four vertices, first is the four vertices at the side of the one column and press "F" as a shortcut in creating faces. Then I select the other four vertices in the side of another column and press F again to create faces. Then select the remaining four vertices that are in the middle of the two columns.

Now, take a look at Figure 2-77 to see the output of what we did in the top of the rook.

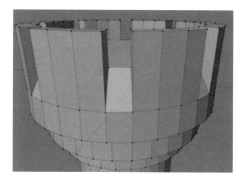

Figure 2-77. *First Phase: Top of Rook piece*

Let's take a look at the current progress of the rook piece as a whole as shown in Figure 2-78.

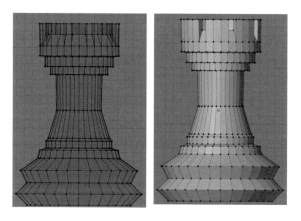

Figure 2-78. *Current progress of Rook piece*

Now I add the subsurface modifier to the rook piece. Again, after adding this modifier, we will need to adjust something to smooth out the mesh. Take a look at Figure 2-79 to see a glimpse of the process of how I did the work in the second phase of modeling with the rook piece.

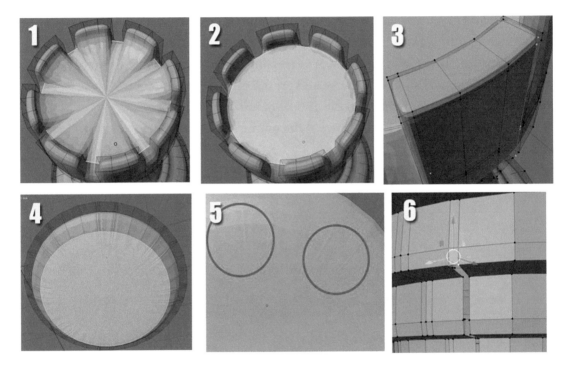

Figure 2-79. *Second Phase of Modeling of Rook piece*

For the second phase, aside from fixing some stuff after I applied the subsurface modifier, I use the inset tool at the top of the rook as you can see in images 1 and 2 of Figure 2-79. I add new loops to create the look I want for the column like you can see in image 3. I also use the inset tool at the bottom of the rook as shown in image 4. This is the same method that we used in the pawn piece.

Okay. Let's discuss a little bit what can make your edges sharp. First is when you add a crease. When you add a crease, yes, you might have sharp edges, but you don't have full control over it. Adding loop cuts and dragging them near to the other loop cuts can also sharpen your edges but also increase vertices.

Now, as you can see in image 5, I encircle part of the bottom of the rook that has unwanted artifacts. These are the effects of the loops I added. It's because the vertices and edges at the bottom of the rook become too close to each other. In order to fix these, you just need to delete some vertices and edges that create only small faces and then replace them with some larger faces as can be seen in image 6.

But I want to note that this is up to you if you want to still fix these small problems – because, for example, your game asset will be placed in the background. Do you think making it too detailed will help? If that bottom part of the rook will not be seen in the game you are creating, will it be necessary for you to take time to fix it that much? This is where what we learn regarding low poly vs. high poly will be useful.

Take a look Figure 2-80 to see the final output in the modeling process of the rook piece.

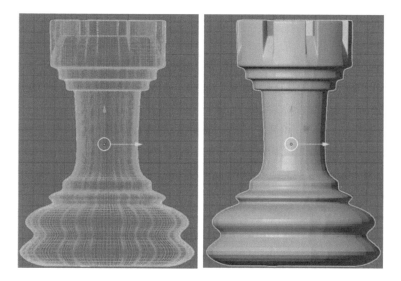

Figure 2-80. *Rook Piece (Left: Wireframe view, Right: Solid view)*

Sample Project - Knight Chess Piece

Let's proceed with the knight piece. We will have a different approach here because it isn't as simple as the first two pieces, but I will only show in figures those highlighted parts of the process. We will now begin.

Take a look at Figure 2-81 to see some highlighted parts of the process.

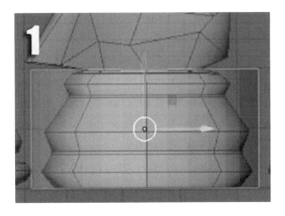 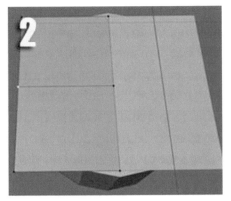

Figure 2-81. *Knight Piece process*

First step, I created the base using the cylinder. For the base, it was the same method with the base of the pawn and the rook. Then it was scaling and extruding, as well as transforming and using the inset tool in the bottom part.

In the top part, the horse head, take a look at Figure 2-81, where things become different. First, from the modeling workplace, I go to object mode and I add a mesh plane object by holding Shift + A ➤ Mesh ➤ Plane. Then, I go back to edit mode and hold Ctrl + R, then enter to create a loop in the plane. For this particular process, I make sure that the loop is in the center. Then, I select the face at the right side of the plane and delete it. Now, I add the mirror modifier, which copies what you do to certain elements. In this way, it will help me do this project easier since I will only worry about the left part. I don't need to worry about the other side.

Take a look at Figure 2-82 to see the settings of the mirror modifier.

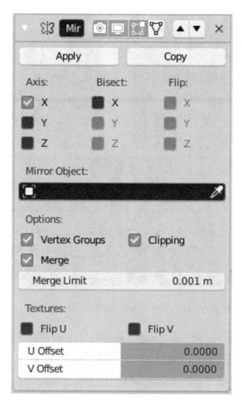

Figure 2-82. *Mirror Modifier*

The settings for axis indicate the axis that will be mirrored. The bisect settings enable you to cut the mesh across the mirror plane. The flip settings flip the direction of the slice. Mirror object is where you can choose a particular object to be mirrored. Clipping prevents the vertices by passing by the mirrored element during the transformation, and merge merges the vertices within the merge threshold. Vertex groups mirror the vertex groups and merge limits indicate the distance of the merge-mirrored vertices. The part under textures are all settings for applying textures in the mirrored vertices.

By default, clipping is unchecked, so I enable it to make sure that I will not go beyond the part of the mirrored elements.

Now take a look at Figure 2-83 to see the other highlighted part of the process.

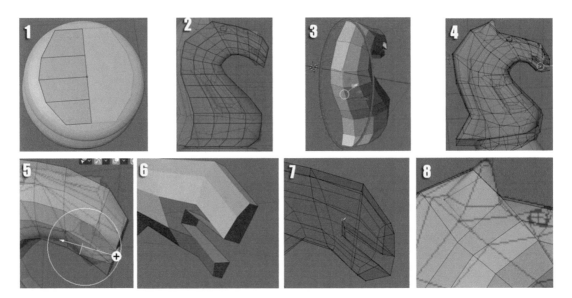

Figure 2-83. *Highlighted process for Knight Piece*

After adding the mirror modifier, I once again use Ctrl + R to create three loops in the plane and form it into a circle that will match the base that I made as you can see in image 1 of Figure 2-83. Then, I extrude and transform, using the move, scale, and rotate tools, the circle you can see in image 2 of Figure 2-83 to form the basic shape of the knight. After that, I select the face at the back of the head and extrude it to form the hair-like part for the knight as you can see in images 3 and 4 of Figure 2-83. Then I select the part of the head that is nearer to the mouth and extrude it toward the inside as you can see in image 5. And since after I extrude this part, it will leave a face outside, at the side part, which is not a lot like a mouth, I deleted the vertices left outside that leave spaces just like you can see in image 6 of Figure 2-83. In order it fill it in, I use the knife tool as you can see in image 7. Then, I add the ears using the knife tool as you can see in image 8 of Figure 2-83.

This process needs a lot of practice for you to be able to achieve your real goal so if at the first attempt you don't make it, don't be frustrated. Just try it again, match and closely look at your reference, and you will be able to achieve.

Now, the second phase begins. I add the subsurface modifier and start adding details as you can see in Figure 2-84.

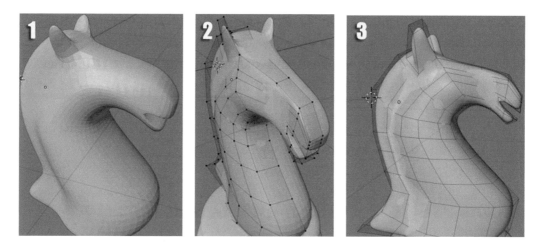

Figure 2-84. *Knight Piece Second Phase*

You might notice that I didn't add eyes. Well, that's part of the creativity aspect. We can add or delete some details as long as the basic or main concept is still there. In this part, we're doing a knight piece. As long as the silhouette or the thing that can make the knight piece is still there, it doesn't matter if we delete some small details like the eyes.

Now, let's take a look at Figure 2-85 to see the final touch in the modeling part of the knight piece.

Figure 2-85. *Knight Piece finale in Modeling (Left: Wireframe view, Right Solid view)*

As you can see in Figure 2-85, in the wireframe view of the knight piece, it seems to have a lot of vertices already. It's the effect of a subsurface modifier. Remember that if you don't need to have that much detail, and your asset doesn't need to be that smooth, just lower your values in the subsurface when you use it because it will also affect your rendering in the end.

Since we have only left the king, queen, and bishop, I will not discuss much of its process since it also has the same methods with the previous chess pieces.

Sample Project - Bishop, Queen, and King

Now, let's take a look at Figure 2-86 to see the process for the bishop piece.

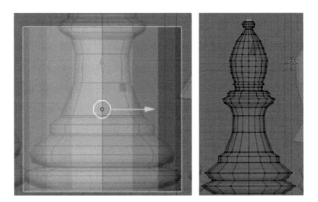

Figure 2-86. *Bishop Piece process*

You can see, after I add a cylinder, I just extrude it, scale, and move vertices, and I already came up with the basic form of the bishop. After I add the subsurface modifier, I just use the inset tool at the bottom and at the top, since we use the cylinder and we need to add another loop in that big circle to minimize the effect of crowded vertices. Then it's already done. Take a look at Figure 2-87 to see the final output in the modeling phase of the bishop piece.

Figure 2-87. *Bishop Piece finale in Modeling (Left: Wireframe view, Right: Solid view)*

Now, let's go with the queen. Take a look at Figure 2-88 to see the process done with the queen chess piece.

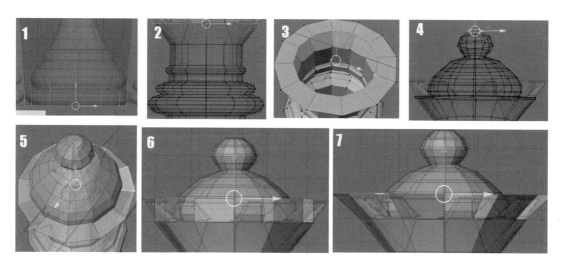

Figure 2-88. *Queen Piece process*

You can notice in Figure 2-88 that the technique I did with the queen piece is the same with the rook. Again, I use the cylinder, transform, extrude, and then when it comes to the crown, I just extrude the top loop just like you can see in image 3 of Figure 2-88, then extrude the faces as you can see in image 5. As long as you have the reference, and you know the basics like vertices, faces, edges, scaling, moving, rotating, and then extruding, you can easily do this modeling. Well, of course, constant practice is a must too.

I'd like to note that I set the segment of the cylinder to just 12 from its settings that show when you add the mesh. That setting cannot be changed when you already move or do an adjustment to your object.

Since the second phase that comes after adding the subsurface modifier is more of a minor edit, let's just proceed and take a look at Figure 2-89 to see the output of all the processes we did for the queen.

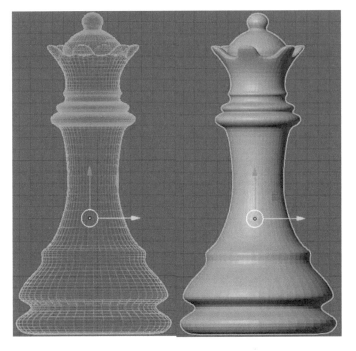

Figure 2-89. *Queen Piece finale in Modeling (Left: Wireframe view, Right: Solid view)*

Then for our last chess piece, we will have the king. Let's take a look at Figure 2-90 to see the process of how the king piece is made.

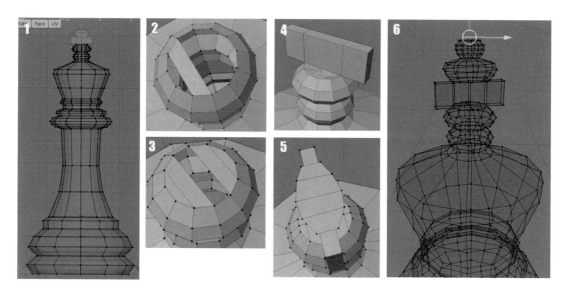

Figure 2-90. *King Piece process*

Again, I just use a cylinder and set its segments to 12. Just using the scale and extrude, I came up with image 1 of Figure 2-90. For me to create the top part of the king piece, I delete the top circle face and reconnect the vertices as you can see in images 2 and 3. I extrude the face at the center to create the cross as you can see in image 4, and then I use the knife tool to create a loop that can help me make the rounded part of the cross like the top of the king piece as you see in image 5. Then, once again, I just highlight the vertices to transform and use extrude and scale to complete what you see in image 6.

Okay, now let's take a look at Figure 2-91 to see the final output in the modeling part of the king piece.

Figure 2-91. *King Piece finale in Modeling (Left: Wireframe view, Right: Solid view)*

Now, we're done with the three remaining chess pieces. We will now proceed to the next chapter, which is about the shading techniques for game assets using Blender. But, before I conclude this chapter, I'd like you to look at Figure 2-92 to see the whole game environment we have for this sample project.

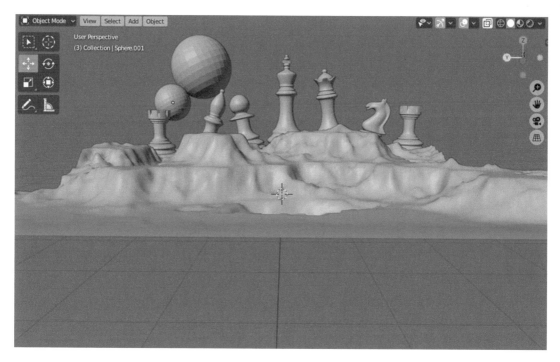

Figure 2-92. *Sample Project Game Environment in Camera Perspective*

So here, I use the add-on landscape that you can enable in preferences by going to Edit menu ➤ Preference ➤ Addons ➤ Add mesh: A.N.T. landscape. This add-on can be found in the sidebar menu of the 3D viewport, which you can also access by pressing "N" on your keyboard.

I just modified some stuff in its settings until I see my preferred setup and here it is. It was just a plain scene for a game environment design. I don't want to create some complex one since what I wanted to tackle was the basics, which we always forgot.

As you can see, most of my chess pieces have high vertices. As you can see in Figure 2-92, although the chess pieces are in the background, I'm making them stand out by enlarging them. When it comes to texturing, the number of vertices will also affect them. And since I want these chess pieces to stand out in the background at least, I want them to have both good geometry and textures.

Now, we'll now start Chapter 3! I hope you continue to enjoy this book.

CHAPTER 3

Color It!

Good day, my dear readers! We're now at Chapter 3.

In the previous chapter, we learned the basics of modeling a game asset and some tips for creating a game environment. In this chapter, we will get started with how to shade and put colors in your game asset to give more life to it. We'll cover color theory and the UV workspace, which allows us to put a 2D image onto a 3D object. The next chapter covers creating your own textures.

Now, without further ado, let's get started!

Color Fundamentals

Before we start our discussion of Blender's features that are related to texturing your game asset, let's first discuss the fundamentals of colors.

Colors are there to enhance your design, not to be your design. Even without them, your asset must show its design. In creating characters for anime or comics, there is this tip by which you can tell that the character has a powerful image or is created with a nice back story if when you black it out or when you can only see the silhouette of that character, you can tell which character it is. I believe this can also be applicable to game assets. You can tell that you created well your game asset if when you black it out, without any color and just its silhouette, you can recognize it apart from other assets.

There's a lot of things to study when it comes to color. We will just discuss some of the important parts that can help us efficiently design a game environment.

Color Theory

Color theory encompasses a multitude of definitions, concepts, and design applications. However, there are three basic categories of color theory that are logical and useful: the color wheel, color harmony, and the context of how colors are used.

© Ezra Thess Mendoza Guevarra 2020
E. T. Mendoza Guevarra, *Creating Game Environments in Blender 3D*,
https://doi.org/10.1007/978-1-4842-6174-3_3

The first color wheel has been attributed to Sir Isaac Newton, who arranged red, orange, yellow, green, blue, indigo, and violet into a natural progression on a rotating disk. As the disk spins, the colors blur together so rapidly that the human eye sees white. From there, the organization of color has taken many forms, from tables and charts to triangles and wheels.

As of now, there is no substantive evidence that supports a universal of color theory.

A color wheel is an abstract illustrative organization of color hues around a circle, which shows the relationship between primary colors, secondary colors, tertiary colors, and so on. The Itten color wheel consist of twelve colors, which are three primary, three secondary, and six tertiary. The influence of psychoanalysis is apparent in Itten's color theory, as he was one of the first to associate different colors with specific emotions and to study the impact of color on our moods.

Discussion about primary colors results in a lot of debates now because of the appearance of different types of color systems. Now, what we called primary colors, secondary colors, and tertiary colors depend on what color system are you using.

Even though I know that you have already seen this wheel many times in your life, I'd like you to take a look at our color wheel in Figure 3-1.

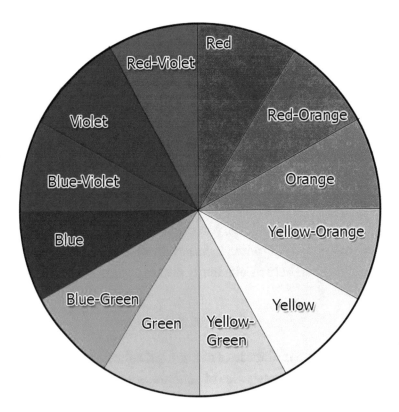

Figure 3-1. Color Wheel

Color Meaning

Colors have different psychological meanings, depending on how you use them. Besides the usual cultural meanings attached to colors, we can even see color personality, which links the meaning of color to an individual's personality. Knowing this, we need to be conscious of what meaning we're conveying. We need to learn how we can use colors appropriately.

It's not the colors themselves that have specific meaning but rather the culturally assigned meanings to them. Since we have culturally assigned meaning to them, it is important to know our target audience so that we can research the meanings of certain colors related to their culture and tradition.

Now, let's talk about the general meaning attached to colors.

- **Warm Colors:** Pertaining to colors like red, orange, and yellow. They are associated with passion, energy, impulsiveness, happiness, coziness, and comfort. They can easily draw attention and have the advantage of being inviting and harmonious.

- **Cool Colors:** Pertaining to colors like blue, green, and violet. They are associated with calm, trust, and professionalism. They are also associated with sadness and melancholy. They do have an advantage of being professional and harmonious but can turn off people by the coolness they radiate.

- **Red:** Color of fire and blood. It is emotionally intense. Associated with energy, war, danger, strength, power, determination, action, confidence, courage, vitality, passion, desire, and love. It can enhance metabolism, increase respiration, and raise blood pressure. Has a high visibility and advances to the foreground. Red is also a magical and religious color. It symbolizes super-human heroism to the Greeks and is the color of the Christian crucifixion. Red was almost as rare as purple in ancient days, a fact that may explain its magic and power. A fun fact about the influence of this color red is the international color for stop, but when you also hear the word "red-light district," it pertains to stores that sell sex and pornography. Red is also the color of good luck in Asia, especially in China; and in East Asian stock markets, red is used to denote a rise in stock prices. But take note, in North American stock markets, red is used to denote a drop in stock prices. Red captures attention. It is one of the most visible colors, second to yellow.

- **Yellow:** Color of the sun. Bright yellow attracts attention, though it can also be distracting when overused. Associated with joy, happiness, wisdom, and intellectual energy. It stimulates mental activity and generates muscle energy. It produces a warming effect and is often used to evoke cheerfulness or pleasant feelings. Shades of yellow can become dingy, lessening the pleasing effect. Yellow is the most luminous of all colors of the spectrum. It's the color that captures our attention more than any other color. Fun facts about the influence of this color are that yellow is the color of traffic lights and signs indicating caution all over the world. In Japan, it represents courage while in China, adult movies are referred to yellow movies (I wonder why). In Russia, a colloquial expression for an insane asylum used to be a yellow house while in some areas in Mexico, bright marigold yellow may be associated with death. Yellow has a high light reflectance value and therefore it acts as a secondary light source.

- **Blue:** Color of the sky and sea. Slows metabolism, breathing, and heart rate. It is also seen as a masculine color. Associated with trust, loyalty, wisdom, intelligence, expertise, confidence, stability, and depth. Creates a calming effect and suppresses appetite and has been considered to be beneficial to both mind and body. Fun facts about this color are that Greeks believe that blue wards off "the evil eye." Dark blue is the color of mourning in Korea. Shades of blue are described as shallow or deep instead of light or dark in China. Also, in Belgium, blue is for baby girl and pink is for baby boy. Lastly, "Prince Charming" is called "The Blue Prince" in Italy and Spain.

- **Orange:** Combines the energy of red with the happiness of yellow. It's not as aggressive as red and calls to mind healthy food. Associated with joy, sunshine, the tropics, enthusiasm, happiness, fascination, creativity, determination, attraction, success, encouragement, stimulation, and strength. Can increase appetite and evokes thoughts of fall and harvest. Fun facts about this color are that it symbolizes autumn. Orange is the color of life rafts, hazard cones, and high-visibility police vests globally. Orange (saffron) is a sacred and auspicious color in Hinduism; and in the United Kingdom, orange stands for the Northern Irish Protestants and has very strong religious and political significance.

- **Green:** Color of nature. It symbolizes growth, hope, freshness, and fertility. In countries with green money such as the United States, it evokes thoughts and feelings of financial wealth. Associates with healing, stability, endurance, harmony, safety, life, and well-being. Sometimes signifies a lack of experience and is often used to indicate the safety of drugs and medical products in advertising. Fun facts about the color green are that in China, green may symbolize infidelity. A green hat symbolizes that a man's wife is cheating on him. In Israel, green may symbolize bad news. In Japan, the words for blue and green, which are "ao" were the same until after World War II when the nihonggo word Midori, which means green, was already thought of as a separate color, not just as a shade of blue.

- **White:** Associated with light, goodness, purity, innocence, and virginity. It usually has positive connotations and is seen as safe and clean.

- **Purple:** Combines the stability of blue and the energy of red. It conveys wealth and extravagance, and it seen as the color of royalty. Symbolizes power, nobility, luxury, and ambition. Associated with wisdom, dignity, independence, creativity, mystery, and magic. This color seldomly occurs in nature and some may consider it artificial. Light purple is seen as feminine. Purple is also popular with children. In Catholic culture, purple is associated with death; while in some Islamic nations, it is associated with prostitution. Also, purple is the most powerful visible wavelength of electromagnetic energy. This explains why purple is associated with supernatural energy and cosmos than with the physical world. Fun facts about this color are that the "Purple Heart" is the American award for bravery. In Italy, most performing artists would not go on stage if they had to wear anything purple. Also, purple is the hardest color for the eye to discriminate.

- **Black:** Associated with power, elegance, formality, death, evil, and mystery. It denotes strength and authority. Seen as formal and elegant, it brings forth feelings of fear and the unknown.

- **Gray:** Color of sorrow, detachment, and isolation. It connotes responsibility and conservative practicality. It's a neutral color and creates noninvasive feelings. Associated with security, maturity, and dependability. It can be used to reduce the intense energy of another color and to emphasize a willingness to comply.

- **Brown:** Color of the Earth. Tends to blend into the background. Associated with material things, order, and convention. Its connection to Earth gives stability. Can convey solid and wholesome feelings.

Usually, warmer colors advance into the foreground while cooler colors reside in the background. It's because warmer colors attract more attention than cooler ones. By mixing warm and cool colors, you can create depth in your design.

Color Harmony

In order to create the best color combination for our design, we need to understand the word **harmony**. By definition, harmony is the combination of simultaneously sounded musical notes to produce chords and chord progressions having a pleasing effect. Applying to colors, color harmony means a combination of colors to produce a balance and pleasing color effect. So, how can we achieve that? We can achieve this by using this term, which is also very familiar with many of us: the **color scheme**.

Color Scheme

There are two ways to create a color scheme. One is with the color scheme that is based on the color wheel; and the one way is that many of us are familiar with: monochromatic, analogous, complementary, etc., and the color scheme based on nature.

Color schemes based on nature are simply color schemes produced from nature itself. It sounds simple, right? Yeah. But creating it was actually a little bit complex. Creating a scheme based on nature involves not just understanding colors but also understanding lighting. We're dealing with nature itself and nature has these unbeatable light sources: sun, moon, and stars. You cannot cut them off.

A color scheme based on nature can also be classified as a custom color scheme. There are other ways to create a custom color scheme; but make note that when creating your own color scheme, you need to keep in mind things like chroma, hue, value, and saturation – creating a custom color scheme means you are not using the formal rules.

Take a look at Figure 3-2 to see a sample of a color scheme based on nature and other custom colors.

Based on Nature

Figure 3-2. *Custom Color Scheme*

As you can see in Figure 3-2, I base the color in a picture on nature, but even though it was based on a picture, or let's say a customized color scheme, I make sure there's still a pattern in my color scheme. You will notice that the shades of my color palette have something to do with green, and then I also choose something with shades of gray. Gray is a neutral color, just like white and black, so it can balance with any color.

Color schemes based on color wheels or traditional color schemes are based on formal rules. There are six types of these color schemes: monochromatic, analogous, complementary, split-complementary, tetradic, and triadic.

Now, let's discuss each of these types.

- Monochromatic Color Scheme

  It looks clean and elegant. Effective at establishing an overall mood. Tends to be very unified and harmonious. It is based on different tones of the same color. It is the simplest color scheme to create, since it was taken from the same color, making it harder to create a jarring or ugly scheme. This scheme is easy to create but can also be boring if it isn't created properly. Adding in a strong neutral like white and black can help keep things interesting.

Take a look at Figure 3-2 to see a sample of a monochromatic scheme.

Based on Blue

Figure 3-3. *Monochromatic Color Scheme*

One thing I notice for a monochromatic color scheme is that in order to balance your color palette, you need to have something like a white color.

- Analogous Color Scheme

  It is similar to a monochromatic scheme, but it offers more nuances as it draws from a wider band on the color wheel. Often found in nature. Harmonious and pleasing to the eye. It can also be very versatile. It is based on colors adjacent to each other on the color wheel. This color scheme is another easy one to create next to a monochromatic color scheme since it was created based on three colors next to each other on the color wheel. In traditional color wheels, analogous have the same chroma level, but by using tones, tints, saturation, values, shades, and lightness, we can add interest to these schemes and make our design more interesting.

  Now, take a look at Figure 3-4 to see our example for an analogous color scheme.

Based on Blue, Blue-Green and Blue-Violet

Figure 3-4. *Analogous Color Scheme*

Playing with different shades, tones, tints, saturations, and values can make this color scheme more interesting!

- Complementary Color Scheme

  This is created by combining colors from opposite sides in the color wheel. It looks best when a warm color is used against a cool color. Creates an intrinsically high level of contrast and creates a dramatic look. The colors intensify each other and are extremely eye-catching and vibrant. I just want to note that using colors with their exact opposites with the same chromas and/or values can be visually jarring.

  Take a look at Figure 3-5 to see our example for a complementary color scheme.

Based on Yellow and Violet

Figure 3-5. *Complementary Color Scheme*

In order to find the better palette for this one, you need to find a good match of color from the color wheel from the start.

- Split-Complementary Color Scheme

  It offers high contrast without the strong tension of complementary colors. It adds more complexity than a regular complementary color scheme. They have more variety then complementary color schemes though they're less vibrant and attention grabbing. Created by choosing one color and then two more colors that are adjacent to the complementary color of the initial color.

  Take a look at Figure 3-6 to see our example for a split-complementary color scheme.

Based on Red, Violet and Green

Figure 3-6. *Split-Complementary Color Scheme*

> This color scheme creates a vibrant feel, but you also need to be careful in choosing your colors and their applications to your design or instead of these colors helping you emphasize your design, they may ruin it.

- Triadic Color Scheme

> It offers a strong visual contrast while still retaining harmony and a richness of color. It can be vibrant even when the colors are unsaturated, and it has stability because each color in the triad balances the other two. Uses three colors equally spaced around the color wheel.

> Now, take a look at Figure 3-7 to see our example for this color scheme.

Based on Blue, Yellow and Red

Figure 3-7. *Triadic Color Scheme*

- Tetradic Color Scheme

> It can be hard to harmonize and may look unbalanced. Makes for a rich color scheme with lots of variation. Created by choosing colors at the corners of a rectangle inscribed on the color wheel.

> Let's take a look at Figure 3-8 to see our example for a tetradic color scheme.

Based on Blue, Violet, Yellow-Green and Yellow-Orange

Figure 3-8. *Tetradic Color Scheme*

Note   To decide your color scheme, you must think of what message you want to convey in your design. Usually, when you decide on a color scheme, you begin with the dominant color.

Colors can be presented in different spaces using different attributes, and these attributes can help us create more pleasing designs. These attributes are the values, hues, saturations, tones, intensities, tints, and chromas.

Hue, Saturation, Values (HSV) and Others

I guess if you know Photoshop, you have already seen this term. It's where you can adjust your hue, saturation, and values that can give some effect in your photo or layout. Let's understand more what these three terms mean for us.

- **Hue** is the actual color of an object. Violet, blue, and red are examples of a hue. Hues can be more specifically described as the dominant wavelength and is the first item we refer to when adding in the three components of color. It essentially refers to a color having full saturation.

- **Saturation** is the degree of purity of a hue. It is similar to chroma, though not quite the same thing. Pure hues are highly saturated. When gray is added, the color becomes desaturated. Saturation defines the brilliance and intensity of a color. When a pigment hue is "toned," both white and black (gray) are added to the color to reduce saturation. It is also described as how much of a given hue is in a filter.

Note   Highly saturated colors or pure hues are perceived as more dynamic, but too many saturated colors can compete and cause eye fatigue. Desaturated colors lend themselves to performance and efficiency. Desaturated bright colors are perceived as friendly and professional, while desaturated dark colors are perceived as serious and professional.

- **Value or Luminance** is a measure of the amount of light reflected from a color and is basically how light or dark a hue is. Adding white to a hue makes it lighter and increases its value or luminance. This can also be said that it is something that refers to the lightness and darkness of a color. It indicates the quantity of light reflected. Adding black lowers the value.

- **Chroma** is the colorfulness of an area being judged as a proportion of the brightness of a similarly illuminated area that appears white or highly transmitting.

Note   Chroma and saturation are often used interchangeably but are defined distinct concepts by the Commission Internationale de l'Eclairage (CIE), whose terminology is widely accepted as standard in science and technology.

- **Intensity** is the brightness or dullness of a color.

- **Shade** is the result of adding black to a hue to produce a darker hue. Shade is equal to pure hue plus black. High saturations have a lot of one particular hue, are very chromatic, and we call colors in that range shades.

- **Tint** is the result of adding white to a hue to produce a lighter hue. Tint equates to a pure hue plus white. Also, tints tend to allow a lot of light to pass through them. Low saturation is closer to a white light and colors in that ranges are called tints.

- **Tone** is the result of adding gray to a hue. Tone is equal to pure hue plus gray.

Note Because all color is relative, nothing is objectively a tint or a shade.

Now that we're done with the color attributes, let's talk about the color system.

Color Systems

What are the color systems? Are they important to discuss? Its description is quite technical but even you aren't an artist, you will encounter color systems. For example, this term is also referred to as RGB. Every gadget we have uses the RGB color system, known to be an additive color system, in order to show us the colors: those printed products, the colors in those products. RGB uses a different color system. Knowing these color systems will make us understand and know when to use such a color palette and the limits of technology. Not only that, understanding the color system will let us know more about the colors themselves and help us manage our design effectively. There's a lot of color systems, but we're discussing only five here: additive color, subtractive, PMS, RYB, and HSL. Let's now start the discussion.

- Additive Color System (RGB)

  This color system is what we usually find in computer monitors, etc., as I mentioned before. RGB stands for red, green, and blue. To create colors on a computer screen, we have to add light since the light source comes from within, instead of reflecting the light coming from the outside of the system. When there is no light, we see black and as we add more color, we move toward white.

  It also be noted that variability with screen brightnesses, lightning conditions, and hue and contrast settings will render the exact same color differently from one computer monitor or gadget's screen to another.

Note Color is light. Light is electromagnetic radiation, and over a range of wavelengths, it makes an impression on the human eye. This range of wavelengths is the visual spectrum. When light hits an object, some wavelengths are absorbed. When all the wavelengths in the visual spectrum are absorbed, we see black. When all are reflected, we see white. When some are absorbed and some are reflected, we see different colors.

- Subtractive Color System (CMYK)

    This color system refers to full-color printing. CMYK stands for cyan, magenta, yellow, and black. When we see colors in physical objects, we're seeing reflective light. When we see red, it's because all the other wavelengths of light have been absorbed and only the red is reflected. This is a subtractive system because in order to produce color, we're removing all the wavelengths of light whose colors we don't want to see. As we add more colors to the system, more light is absorbed and the overall color gets darker. Subtractive systems start with white and continue to add color until the result is black.

    Let's take a look at Figure 3-9 to see the chart that can reflect the RGB and CMYK color systems.

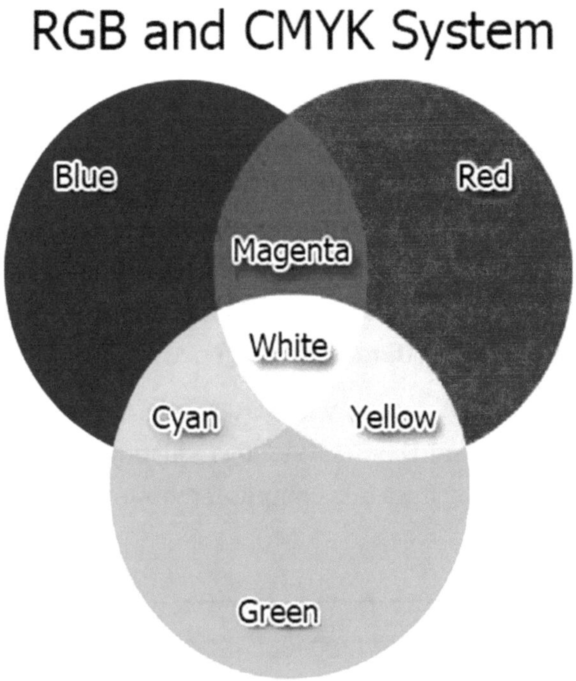

Figure 3-9. *RGB and CMYK system*

- Pantone Matching System (PMS)

This is a system of thousands of numbered swatches. Most corporate colors, like logos, are identified with a number from this system. Pantone colors are also called spot colors.

This is similar to picking paint or hardware because you refer to the swatches of colors. It can be used both digitally and in prints.

Take a look at Figure 3-10 to see a sample of a Pantone code and color.

Pantone PMS 19-4052
Classic Blue
#0f4c81

Figure 3-10. *PMS Color system*

- RYB Color System

RYB stands for red, yellow, and blue. It is the basic among the basics. Oh, what does it mean? It is usually the first color system we learned when we were young, though I don't know if all of us have the same experience with it; but for most it's a yes. It is like how mixing blue and yellow can produce the color green.

The concept of RYB and RGB lies in the perspective at which light comes to you. RYB is more applicable in traditional arts like painting since the concept of paint is that color absorbs every color but one that is reflecting. This means that red absorbs every color except red, blue absorbs every color except blue, and yellow absorbs every color except yellow. In this case, when you add colors together, what you are doing is adding to the amount of colors that the paint will absorb. You can also call this a subtractive color system because when you add different colors together, what you are actually doing is subtracting the amount of light that the paint can reflect.

- HSL Color System

    Although the RGB system can easily help us generate colors, they are not recommended for us artists to use. Instead, HSL or hue, saturation, and lightness is the one we use for finding the right color for our design. In the hue/saturation wheel, the angle around the circle defines the hue and the radius defines the saturation. Then, how we can see the lightness? It depends on the slider of the software you are using.

    Take a look at Figure 3-11 to see an example of a hue/saturation wheel.

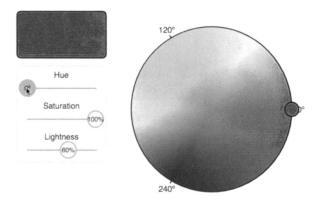

Figure 3-11. *Hue/Saturation Color Wheel*

You can see in Figure 3-11 that this hue/saturation color wheel is the same as the color wheel we see in most digital art software. Just like I said before, it was the recommended system for us. Let's try to understand it further.

First, how is the HSL setting converted to the RGB system, which is perceived in that cube? We should think about the location of the gray color. The tip on finding the location of the gray in the RGB is that anywhere where the RGB values are equal means gray. For example, red = 30, green = 30, blue = 30 or red = 50, green = 50, blue = 50. Then if you visualize this cube and rotate it a little, you will see something familiar and see a color wheel. Take a look at Figure 3-12 to see what I mean by this.

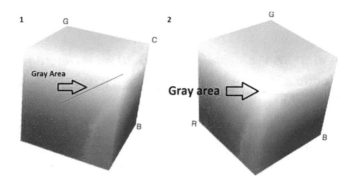

Figure 3-12. *RGB Cube conversion to HSL*

I guess you already feel cheated by scientists and mathematicians here, right? Well, they do lots of formulas in order to create this one but let's leave it out here for now. We're just into the fundamentals of color in this section.

The concept of the lightness in the hue/saturation wheel is like this: Think of that Hue/Saturation circle as a 3D object. Extend that circle into a cylinder. The lightness defines what slice we take out from that cylinder. If it was 50 percent, you take it out at the middle of the cylinder. If you want a lighter color, you need to move up the lightness of that cylinder, and if you want it to be darker, you will move down the cylinder. If 0 percent means a dark color, 100 percent means a brighter color, so what kind of effect do you think the color has if you gave lightness a value of 50 percent? I'll let you think about it.

Note   A small dose of color that contrasts with your main color will draw attention and also make sure to use a variety of tones, values, and levels of saturation for the sake of people with limited color vision.

We are now done with the color fundamentals. Next stop, we'll start to discuss the technical stuff, Blender stuff.

UV Workspace

There are two ways in applying a shade in your mesh. One is using nodes with shader workspace and the other is by using textures or images. When applying these textures and images, or baking textures, you need to do this UV mapping process so that your 3D software can convert the 2D images you are importing as part of the 3D world. This is where the UV workspace is useful.

What then is UV mapping? UV mapping is a process of translating a 3D surface with volume and shape onto a flat 2D texture image. This is necessary in order for you to accurately flatten your custom texture into your 3D model, whether it was made in Blender or coming from the outside. Hmmm, are you confused? Then take a look at Figure 3-13 for you to have a clear visualization of how UV mapping works.

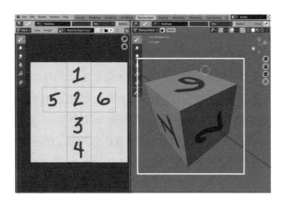

Figure 3-13. *Left: UV Layout, Right: Mesh Cube*

I add a texture so it can easily understand what's going on here. What you can see in the left side, which is also inside the red rectangle, is the UV layout. Blender created the UV layout from our mesh cube using the UV workspace's UV editor. You can think of it like smoothly cutting of the cube in order to make it a flat one so we can prepare it for texturing.

Now, we already know the concept of UV mapping. Let's take a glimpse of the default layout of Blender YV workspace in Figure 3-14.

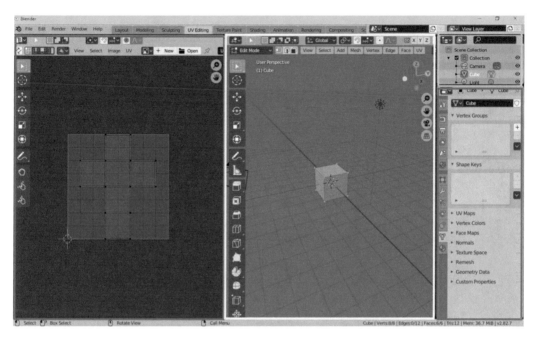

Figure 3-14. *UV Workspace: UV Editor (Red), 3D Viewport(Yellow), Outliner(Green), Properties(Violet)*

We have four editors present in the UV workspace: the UV editor, the 3D viewport, the properties, and the outliner. Let's start with the 3D viewport.

3D Viewport in UV Workspace

3D viewport is available in almost all workspaces except in video editing, masking, rendering, and compositing workspaces. The differences are just its default setup just like what you can see in Figure 3-15.

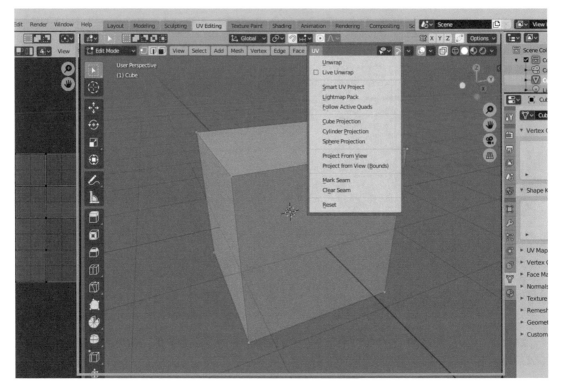

Figure 3-15. *3D viewport default setup in UV workspace*

As you can see, the default setup of 3D viewport is in edit mode and solid shading. For this part, our discussion will be focusing on the one that is inside the red rectangle, which is the UV menu since it's the only one directly related to the features of UV mapping that are in a 3D viewport.

In the UV menu, you can see that we have thirteen tools: Unwrap, Live Unwrap, Smart UV Project, Lightmap Pack, Follow Active Quads, Cube Projection, Cylinder Projection, Sphere Projection, Project from View, Project from View (Bounds), Mark Seam, Clear Seam and Reset. Let's start with Unwrap.

Unwrap

Unwrap is for unwrapping the mesh or element of the object that is currently edited or selected. This means, it is for flattening our mesh. For you to clearly understand this, take a look at Figure 3-16.

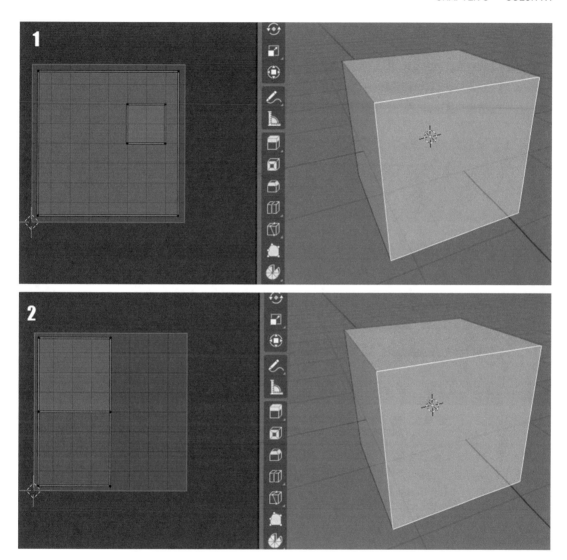

Figure 3-16. *Unwrap at work*

We can see in Figure 3-16 how unwrap tool works. In image 1, the top photo, the unwrap tool isn't used yet. As you can see, there are things overlapping in the UV layout. This kind of UV layout can cause a problem when we do our texturing, especially UV layouts are also been exported to be used in game engines. In image 2, we can see how the unwrap tool fix the problem of the overlapping.

Unwrap tool is the basic tool for UV mapping. You just need to select the part where you want to put your texture and then click unwrap, but this tool also takes a lot of time, especially when it was used in complicated mesh. That's why we have another tool which is called Live Unwrap.

Live Unwrap

Live unwrap changes its UV layout depending on the changes you made in the edge seams of the mesh. Now, take a look at Figure 3-17 and Figure 3-18 to see a little demonstration of how this tool works.

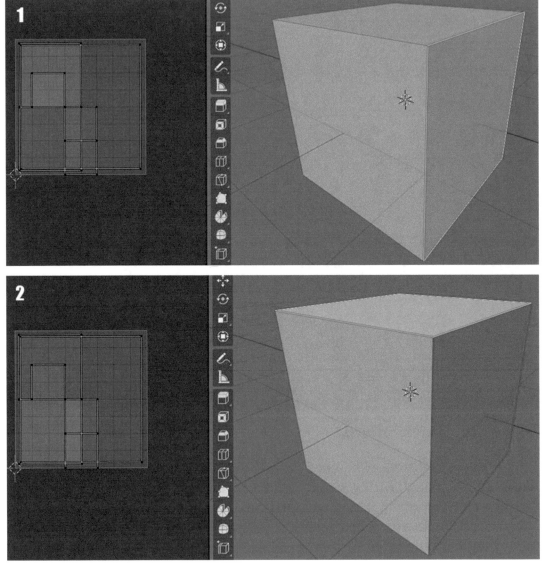

Figure 3-17. *Without Live Unwrap*

You can see here that without using the live unwrap, after we add the seam (which are the red marks in the edges of the cube), nothing changes in the UV layout of our cube unless you unwrap it again. Without live unwrap, what you will always do is add seams and then unwrap them again after adding the seams, which will slow you down when doing it with complicated meshes.

Now, let's take a look at Figure 3-18 where we use the live unwrap.

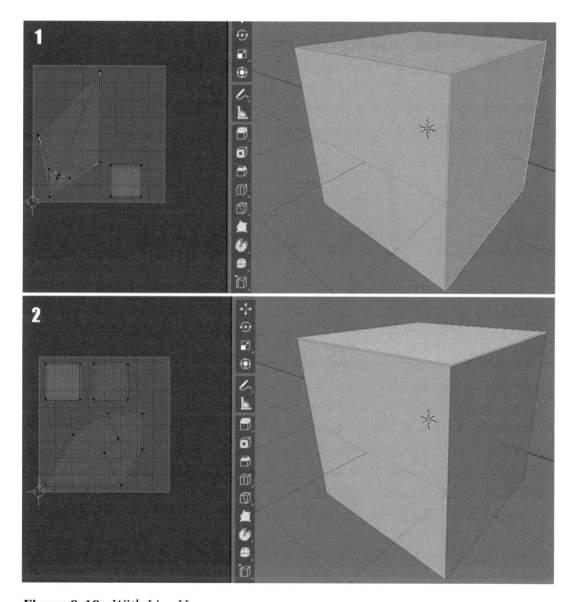

Figure 3-18. *With Live Unwrap*

You can see here an automatic change in the UV layout as we add seams. This is how live unwrap helps us speed up our project.

But what if I want to make a UV layout in an easy and faster way than what we have above? Well, we have that. It's the purpose of Smart UV Project.

Smart UV Project

Smart UV project is a script projection that unwraps the selected faces of a mesh. It operates on all selected mesh objects, and it can be used to unwrap selected faces or all faces. Before this, it was called an archimapper. It examines the shape of your object, the faces selected, and their relation to one another, and then creates a UV map based on this information and settings that we give.

This tool has its own setting as you can see in Figure 3-19.

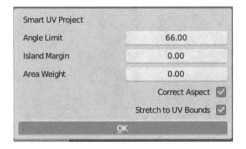

Figure 3-19. *Smart UV Project Settings*

In Smart UV project settings, what we have are Angle Limit, Island Margin, Area Weight, Correct Aspect, and Stretch to UV Bounds.

The **angle limit** controls how faces are grouped. Indicating a higher value will create many small groups of faces but less distortion while indicating a lower value creates a few groups of faces and more of distortion. The **island margin** controls how closely UV islands, or the squares you can see in the UV layout/UV map, are packed together. Zero means no spaces between the UV islands and as the number increases, space increases too.

Take a look at Figure 3-20 to see the effect of the island margin.

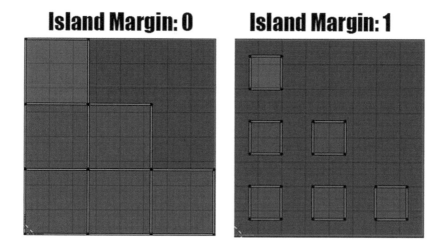

Figure 3-20. *Island Margin at work*

You can see at Figure 3-20 the effect of its value. It is recommended to use a value more than 0 for margins for islands. It will help you with baking and texture bleeding. The margin is a buffer for mipmaps in games and the bakes need a little extra room to fill in the areas between islands. Even when you use texture paint, you will need to bake the maps afterward.

Area weight is the weight projection's vector by faces with larger areas. **Correct aspect** is enabled by default. As long as it was enabled, The map UVs will take the image aspect ratio into account in the process of mapping. Lastly, **stretch to UV bounds,** which is also enabled by default, stretches the final output to texture bounds.

Let's now discuss our fourth tool we have in 3D viewport for our UV, which is the lightmap pack.

Lightmap Pack

Lightmap pack packs each faces UVs into the UV bounds. These are used primarily in a gaming context, where lighting information is baked onto texture maps, when it is essential to utilize as much as UV space as possible. It can also work in several meshes at once. Just like Smart UV project, it also has its own settings. Take a look at Figure 3-21 to see the settings of lightmap pack.

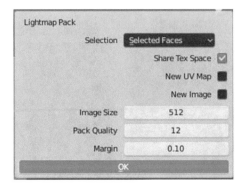

Figure 3-21. *Lightmap Pack Settings*

What we have in Lightmap Pack settings are Selection, which contains Selected Faces and All Faces, Share Tex Space, New UV Map, New Image, Image Size, Pack Quality, and Margin.

Selection is where you can choose if the mapping will be *Selected Faces* or *All Faces*. **Share tex space** is used to attempt to fit all of the objects' faces in the UV bounds without overlapping. It is useful if you're mapping more than one mesh. **New UV map** creates a new UV map for each mesh when mapping multiple meshes. Take a look at Figure 3-22 to see how share tex space works with these multiple meshes.

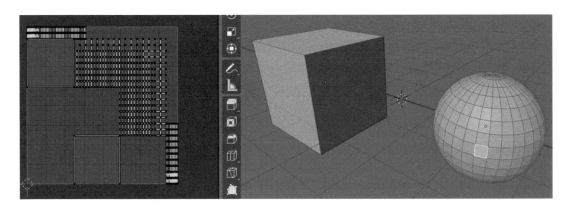

Figure 3-22. *New UV Map*

You can see in Figure 3-22 that there is no overlapping UV island in the UV layout and it was neatly placed in the UV editor. This was thanks to the share tex space settings for lightmap pack.

New image assigns a new image for every mesh but only if shared tex space is enabled. **Image size** sets the size of the image. **Pack quality** does prepacking before the more complex box packing, and **margin** controls how closely the UV islands are packed together. Higher values will add more spaces between the islands.

Wait, for sure you are wondering what does "packing" mean in pack quality? Okay, then. Packing quality controls how efficiently laid-out UV islands are on the texture. Low-pack quality means more texture space but faster unwrap while high-pack quality means the UV islands are better optimized and can use the entire texture but has a slower unwrapping time.

So, now let's move on to the fifth tool, which is follow active quads.

Follow Active Quads

Follow active quads follows UVs from active quads along continues face loops. This tool takes the selected faces and lays them out by the following continues face loops, even if the mesh face is irregularly shaped. It does not respect the image size so you may might have to scale them to fit the image area. Just to be clear, the active quads that are being followed here are the active quads in the UV space, not in the 3D space.

Just like Smart UV project and lightmap pack, they also have their own settings. Take a look at Figure 3-23 to catch a glimpse of them.

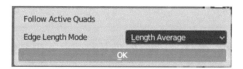

Figure 3-23. *Follow Active Quads settings*

As you can see in Figure 3-23, follow active quads only have simple settings. Their edge length mode settings set the mode on how the UV space will be calculated. They have two options: even and length and length average. **Even** means the UVs will space evenly, and **length average** means the average space of the UVs' edge length of each loop, and this is the default one to use. **Length** is the same as length average.

Take a look at Figure 3-24 to see how follow active quads work.

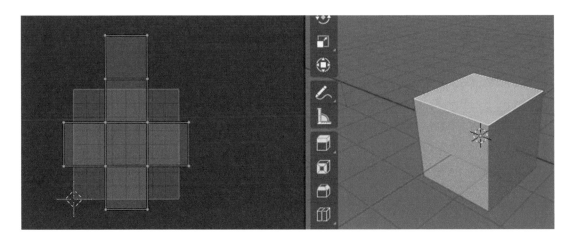

Figure 3-24. *Follow Active Quads at work*

You cannot see many effects if you will look at it them in UV workspace but, you can clearly see their effects when you apply a texture, even just a simple image texture.

Okay, as you can see in Figure 3-24, our UV layout is taking space even outside the image area. That is the reason why we need to scale it down to fit in the area. Sometimes, you will see an error that there is no selected face. Remember that this tool focuses only on the selected faces, so make sure you are selecting it by faces, not by vertices or edges.

Note   The actual creation of UVs are done through a projection technique. Think of it as a projector showing a movie on a screen. The concept is the same, except in a 3D application like Blender, there are different UV projection types available to you. These are based on single geometric shapes and oftentimes are a great starting point to lay out UVs for a single object.

Now, let's proceed to our next tool, which is cube projection.

Cube Projection

Cube projection projects the UV vertices of the mesh over the six faces of a cube, which is then unfolded. It projects the mesh onto the six separates planes, creating six UV islands.

Take a look at Figure 3-25 to see the settings for this tool.

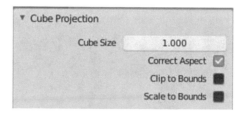

Figure 3-25. *Cube Projection settings*

What we can see on Cube Projection settings are Cube Size, Correct Aspect, Clip to Bounds and Scale to Bounds. First, let's talk about cube size.

Cube size sets the size of the cube to be projected onto. **Correct aspect,** when enabled, will take an image aspect ratio into consideration during UV mapping. **Clip to bounds** makes sure that any UVs that lie outside the 0 to 1 range will be clipped to that range by being moved to the UV space border it is closest to. Last, **scale to bounds** scales a UV map larger than the 0 to 1 range to fit inside.

Just like in the follow active quads, the effect of this tool cannot be felt in UV workspace but in texture workspace, so let's take a look at Figure 3-26.

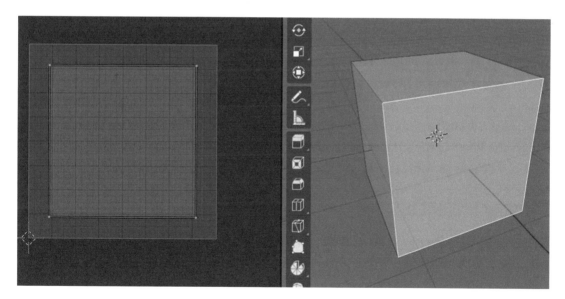

Figure 3-26. *Cube Projection at work in UV workspace*

Figure 3-27 shows how this tool works in both the UV workspace and texture workspace.

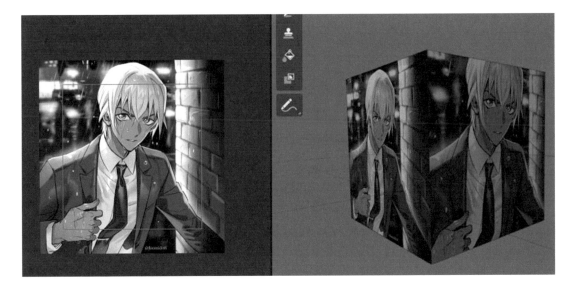

Figure 3-27. *Cube Projection at work in Texture workspace*

As you can see in Figure 3-26, I select the face in the UV editor and scale it down. You can see its effect in Figure 3-27. The other image, where the UV face that we scaled down is linked, gives an impact that it was much closer than the other one. You can also notice that I only select one face for cube projection. I did that to show you some differences that you can notice in Figure 3-27. You can notice it in my mesh cube; even though the two faces have the same image textures, they do have different layouts. The reason is because of how we apply the cube projection and its settings. You should see that in the face I select for cube projection, the image texture seems to be closer than the other one. That is the effect of the smaller cube size.

So, let's now proceed to the next tool, which is the cylinder projection.

Cylinder Projection

Cylinder projection projects the UV vertices of the mesh over the curved wall of the cylinder. It is the same way in the cube projection. The difference is that this is for a cylinder while the other is for a cube.

Take a look at Figure 3-28 to see its settings.

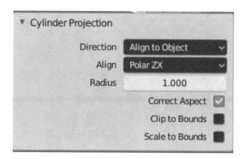

Figure 3-28. *Cylinder Projection settings*

What we can see in Cylinder Projection settings are Direction, Align, Radius, Correct Aspect, Clip to Bounds, and Scale to Bounds.

Direction is to indicate how the UV layout, or the texture that will be used on in the mesh, will be viewed. It has three options: View on Equator, View on Poles, and Align to Object.

View on equator is used if the view is looking at the equator by using a vertical axis. **View on poles** is used when viewing from the top by using an axis that is straight down from the view, and **align to object** if used when you want to calculate the axis base on the object.

Align settings select which axis is up. It has two options, which are **Polar XY,** which sets Polar 0 on the X-axis; and **Polar ZY,** which sets Polar 0 on the Y-axis.

Radius setting sets the radius of the cylinder to use. Once again, since these three are already discussed in the cube projection, **correct aspect**, when enabled, will take the image aspect ratio into consideration during UV mapping. **Clip to bounds** makes sure that any UVs that lie outside the 0 to 1 range will be clipped to that range by being moved to the UV space border it is closest to. Last, **scale to bound** scales a UV map larger than the 0 to 1 range to fit inside.

Take a look at Figure 3-29 to see how a cylinder projection works in a UV workspace.

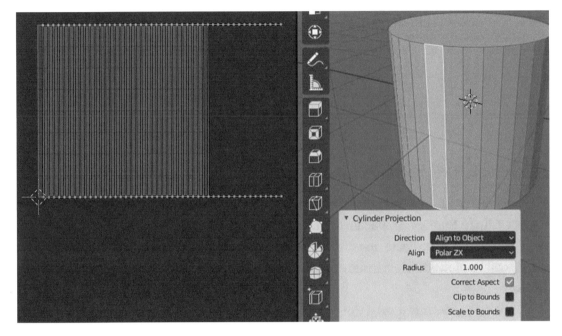

Figure 3-29. *Cylinder Projection at work in UV Workspace*

Figure 3-30 shows its effect on texture through the texture workspace.

Figure 3-30. *Cylinder Projection at work in Texture Workspace*

I used align to object as my direction and you can see its effect in the UV layout. Because the UV islands that represent the top and bottom part of the cylinder are outside the image area and there are also overlapping UV islands, you can see in Figure 3-30 the effect on the texture. Of course, this is just showing you that even though these tools seem to be shortcuts that can help you make your project a lot easier, don't forget about the minor details that can have big effects in the future. When we are in the UV editor part and in the sample project, we will discuss how these problems will be solved.

Sphere Projection

Sphere projection projects the UV vertices of the mesh over the curved surface of a sphere. Its function is like the first two, cube and cylinder projection, but again for sphere. Its settings are almost the same as cylinder projection except that it doesn't have settings for radius.

Now, let's proceed to the next tool, which is the project from view.

Project from View

Project from view projects the UV vertices of the mesh as seen in the current 3D view. It takes the current view in the 3D viewport and flattens the mesh as it appears in the UV map.

Take a look at Figure 3-31 to see its settings.

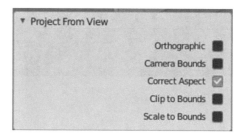

Figure 3-31. *Project from View settings*

What we have here as the settings of Project from View are Orthographic, Camera Bounds, (and the popular three) Correct Aspect, Clip to Bounds, and Scale to Bounds.

Orthographic applies an orthographic projection when enabled. **Camera bounds** maps UVs to the camera region taking resolution and aspect into consideration. **Correct aspect**, when enabled, will take the image aspect ratio into consideration during UV mapping. **Clip to bounds** makes sure that any UVs that lie outside the 0 to 1 range will be clipped to that range by being moved to the UV space border it is closest to. Last, **Scale to bounds** scales a UV map larger than the 0 to 1 range to fit inside.

Take a look at Figure 3-32 to see how project from view works.

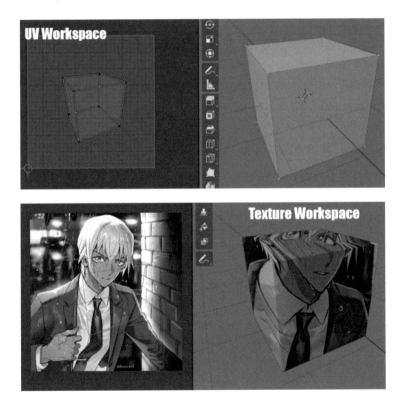

Figure 3-32. *Project from View at work*

You can see in Figure 3-32 how exactly project from view copies the 3D view of the mesh to its UV layout, and you can see its effect on the texture. This is recommended if you use a real-life photo and you want to make it 3D.

Project from view (bounds) works the same as project from view except that scale to bound is already enabled by default.

Let's now move on to mark seam.

Mark Seam

First, what it a seam? If you will think of it like sewing, this is the mark where we put the cloth together. But for unwrapping, this mark indicates where the mesh will be unwrapped. It's like cutting of your mesh. And just a note, the more seams you have, the less stretching there is, but it can affect the texturing process. It's better to have least stretching but at the same time few seams.

You can mark seams by selecting an edge where you want to mark the cut and then hold **Ctrl + E** or by just going to the UV menu and clicking mark seam. After doing this, you will notice a red line on the edge you select to as you can see in Figure 3-33.

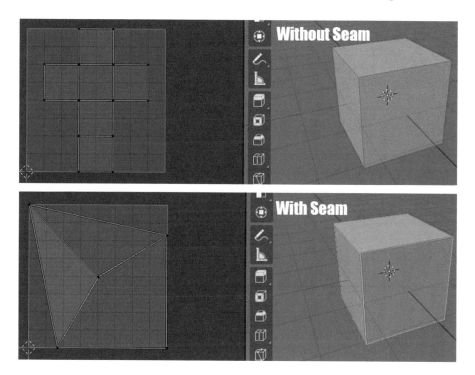

Figure 3-33. *Mark Seam at work*

Depending on where you put your seam, it also affects the UV layout of your mesh and what will happen to your texture.

Next will be **clear seam**, which is obviously used to clear all the marks of the seam in the mesh; and last, **reset**, which resets the UV projection and each face to fill the UV grid, giving the face the same mapping.

We're now done with the features of UV that can be found in the 3D viewport. Now, let's move on to the UV editor.

The UV Editor of UV Workspace

This is the heart of the UV workspace. This is where all the UV mapping happens and where you can edit your UV layout.

Take a look at Figure 3-34 to see the default setup of the UV editor.

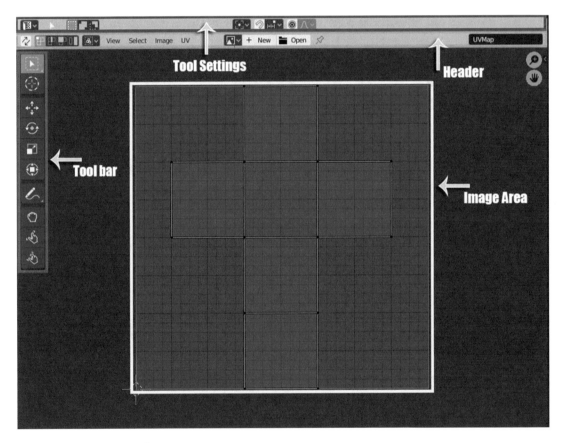

Figure 3-34. UV Editor

The UV editor is divided into three regions: Image area, Toolbar, and Header. The tool settings are not specific to UV editor but they have an important role related to the toolbar. It also has a side bar that can be found in the left side when you press "N" on your keyboard, but by default, it was hidden.

The **image area** is simply the area where you can see the UV layout and edit it. This where the UV mapping process happens.

Now, let's proceed with the UV editor's toolbar together with the tool settings.

UV Editor's Toolbar and the Tool Settings

Unlike in other workspaces like modeling and layout, the settings of the tools that can be seen in the tool settings aren't the same as the settings that can be seen in the pop-up menu settings of a tool. And only move, rotate, scale and transform have pop-up menu settings.

Take a look at Figure 3-35 to see both the toolbar and the settings of each tool that can be found in the tool settings bar.

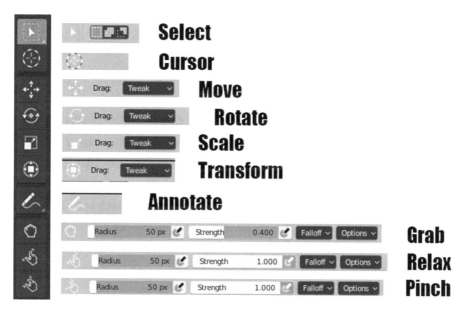

Figure 3-35.   *The toolbar and tool settings for different tools*

The tools that we have here are the Select, Cursor, Move, Rotate, Scale, Transform, Annotate, Grab, Relax, and Pinch – but wait. If you will notice, there are small triangles for Select tool and Annotate. Remember what it means? Yes. There is a pop-up menu that holds other options for this tool. Now that this is already clear, let's start discussing the tools of the UV editor.

First stop is the selection tool, which is by default set in with **box select tool.** This selection tool can help you select the UV vertices in a box selection way. There are three other options there. They are the **tweak tool**, which is the simple form of selection; **circle select tool**, which selects the UV vertices using the circle selection way; and **lasso select tool**, which selects the UV vertices using the lasso selection.

You cannot see any settings for the tweak tool. For the box select and lasso select, they have the same settings.

Take a look at Figure 3-36 to have a closer look at the settings of box select and lasso select, which are for mode selection.

Figure 3-36. *Box Select and Lasso Select settings*

The first box from the right side is the default mode. This means it's just the normal selection mode. When you enable the one in the middle, if you have a current selection of UV vertices and you use your selection tool, it will not affect the current but only extend the existing selection. When you enable the one on the rightmost side, if you have a current selection and you use your selection tool, it will deselect the current selected UV vertices.

The circle select tool has the same settings as the box and lasso select tools with a few differences because it has a setting for radius. This setting for radius affects the cursor circle of the circle select tool.

Now, let's proceed to the other tools we have like **cursor tool**, which sets the cursor location; **move tool**, which moves any selected elements; **rotate tool**, which rotates any selected elements; **scale tool**, which scales any selected element; and **transform tool**, which has the combination of scale, rotate, and move tool.

The cursor tool doesn't have any settings while move, rotate, scale, and transform have similar simple settings.

Take a look at Figure 3-37 to see the settings of these four tools that can be found in the tool settings bar.

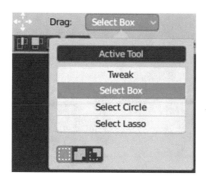

Figure 3-37. *Move, Rotate, Scale, and Transform settings in Tool settings bar*

You can see in Figure 3-37 that its settings are quite simple. It only has four selections for what selection tool you will use and what mode selection you want to apply. By default, they have box selection.

We also have four options for Annotate: Annotate, Annotate Line, Annotate Polygon, and Annotate Eraser. **Annotate** is the basic one and helps you make notes in your project. **Annotate line** helps you create notes including lines. **Annotate polygon** helps you create notes including shapes; and **annotate eraser** helps you undo or erase all of the annotation you made in your projects.

Now, we're already into these three tools that are specific to UV editor: Grab, Relax, and Pinch. I said "specific to UV editor" since those previous tools I mention, though they are part of the tools in UV editor, can be found in other editors or workspaces like in modeling and layout.

Grab, relax, and pinch both sculpt UV vertices using brush. The only difference lies in its effect. The **grab brush/tool** moves the UV vertices around. **Relax brush/tool** makes UVs more evenly distributed, while the **pinch brush/tool** moves UVs toward the brush's center.

Let's take a look at Figure 3-38 to see the settings for these tools.

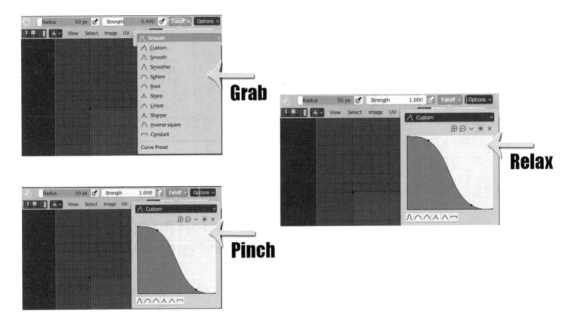

Figure 3-38. *Grab, Relax, and Pinch settings*

You can see in Figure 3-38 that grab settings have a slight difference in the settings of relax and pinch, but overall, they have similar settings. Let's start discussing these settings.

Radius controls the radius of the brush and it is measured in pixels. You can also change the radius by pressing "F" on the keyboard, and then just drag your mouse to any direction and you can see its effect on the red circle (or the radius).

- **Size Pressure** (the icon beside the radius) is for enabling brush sensitivity for size when using a graphic tablet.

- **Strength** controls how much each application of the brush affects the UVs. You can also change the strength by holding "Shift + F," and then, the same with the radius, just drag your mouse to any direction.

- **Strength Pressure** (the icon beside the strength) is for enabling brush sensitivity for strength when using a graphic tablet.

- **Falloff** allows you to control the strength falloff of the brush. The falloff is mapped from the center of the brush, which is the left part of the curve, toward its borders, which is the right part of the curve. Changing the shape of the curve can make the brush softer or harder.

Options contain three selections for UV sculpting. These are **lock borders**, which locks the boundary of UV islands from being affected by the brush when enabled; **sculpt all islands**, which when enabled will allow you to edit all islands and not only the islands nearest to the brush center when the sculpt stroke was started; and **display cursor**, which hides the sculpt cursor when enabled.

Take a look at Figure 3-39 to see how grab, relax, and pinch work.

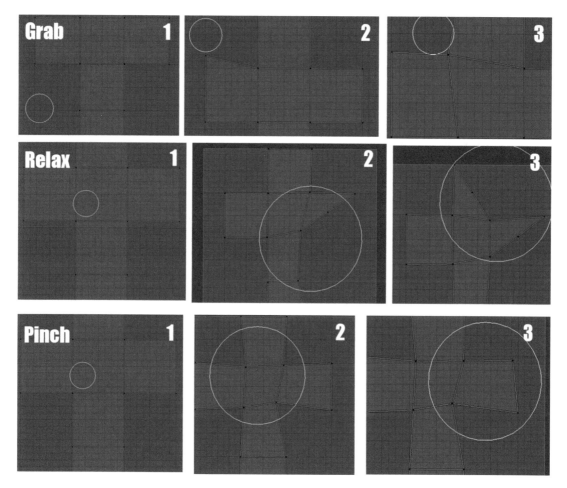

Figure 3-39. *Grab, Relax, and Pinch at work*

You can see that in grab, the UV vertices were just simply moving, with the brush effect. In the relax tool, you can see that the UV vertices are getting separated slowly from each other while in the pinch tool, the vertices are moving toward each other.

Last, we have these three icons in the middle of the tool settings with a drop-down menu, which is the same as shown in Figure 3-40.

Figure 3-40. *Pivot, Snapping, Proportional Editing*

From the left side, we have settings for pivot, snapping, and proportional editing.

Pivot settings are used for you to manipulate the UV islands in an easier way. We have four options here: Bounding Box Center, Median Point, 2D Cursor, and Individual Origins. Unlike when you use pivot in objects and in the 3D viewport, you cannot see much of the effect of pivot or the effect of the pivot isn't visible enough in the UV islands. Since we don't have any "center," the orange dot in UV islands indicates its center.

Snapping settings are used for you to set snapping when editing the UV vertices. Snapping is helpful in allowing you to easily align vertices to each other within a desired parameter. We have two options here: Increments and Vertex. When you choose **increments**, it will snap to increments of a grid while **vertex** will snap to vertices. You can also choose this in settings if the snapping settings will affect the move tool, rotate tool, or scale tool.

Proportional editing settings are sets of options of falloff types. I already mentioned before that falloff is mapped from the center of the brush (or tool), which is the left part of the curve, toward its borders, which is the right part of the curve; and changing the shape of the curve can make the effect of the brush, or the tool you are using; like move, softer; or harder. We already have predefined curved as choices here: Smooth, Sphere, Root, Inverse, Sharp, Linear, Constant, and Random.

Take a look at Figure 3-41 to see how these proportional editing options work.

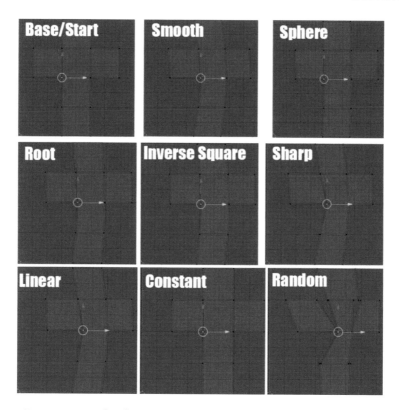

Figure 3-41. *Proportional Editing at work in UV islands*

By default, these three are disabled. So, it's up to you if you will use these tools for your UV mapping process or not.

Now, we're already done with the toolbar and its tool settings. Let's now move on to the header!

UV Editor's Header

Now, let's start discussing the tools that we can see in the header of the UV editor. Let's once again catch a glimpse of this header in Figure 3-42.

Figure 3-42. *UV Editor's Header*

Starting from the left side, we have Sync Selection, Selection Modes, Sticky Selection Modes, View Menu, Select Menu, Image Menu, UV Menu, a drop-down menu for selecting textures, new button, open button, image pin, and Active UV loop layer.

- **Sync selection** keeps the UV and mesh part selections in sync.

- **Selection modes** help you choose how you will edit your UV islands, if by vertices, by edge, by faces or by UV islands.

- **Sticky selection modes** controls how the UVs are selected when the sync selection is disabled.

- **Active UV loop layer** displays the current UV map you are editing.

Now, let's take a look at each header menu that we have. First, let's talk about the view menu.

- In **View** menu, there are many self-explanatory options. I'll just talk about some of the more useful ones here. **Frame Selected** helps you easily zoom in to your selected element. You can also do this by pressing "Numpad."

- **Frame All** helps you easily zoom out or go back to the normal view or the default view of the UV editor. You can also do this by pressing the "Home" key on your keyboard.

- **Frame All Fit** will frame all and fit it to your screen. It's like the easiest way of zooming in. You can also do this by holding "Shift + home."

- **Center View to Cursor** will turn the center of the view to where your current 3D cursor is locating.

- Last, **Area** is for how you want your UV editor to be customized. It has five options: **horizontal split**, where it will split the UV editor into two UV editors horizontally; **vertical split**, where it will split the UV editor into two UV editors vertically; **duplicate area into new window**, where Blender will open another window with UV editor in it; **toggle maximize area**, where Blender will maximize the area of the UV editor and hide other editors that are in the UV workspace like Outliner, Properties, and 3D viewport; and **Toggle Fullscreen Area**, where Blender will have the UV editor take up the full screen, hiding everything except the image area by default.

Let's move on to the next header menu, which is the Select Menu. Here are some of the less-obvious options:

- **Box Select Pinned** (Ctrl + B), which allows you to have a box selection with pinned UV vertices

- **Less** (Ctrl Numpad -), which deselects the UV vertices at the boundary of each selection region.

- **More** (Ctrl Numpad +), which selects more UV vertices connected to the initial selection.

- **Selected Pinned** (Shift P), which selects all pinned UV vertices.

- **Select Linked** (Ctrl L), which selects all UV vertices that are linked to the active UV map.

- **Select Split**(Y), which selects only entirely selected faces.

- **Select Overlap**, which selects overlapping UV vertices.

You might notice that mostly, those in the header menus are common tools/commands that can be seen the workspaces. These are only some specifics, but still, for the sake of at least a review, I will briefly discuss these header menus.

Now let's proceed to the most interesting item on the Image menu. **Open Cached Render** (Alt + R) means reading all the current scene's view layers from cache.

Last, we have the UV menu. I'll only cover a few of these commands, the rest being mostly familiar to you now. First is **transform**. What we have here are options for transforming elements like Move (G), Rotate (R), Resize (S), and Shear (Shift Ctrl Alt S). **Mirrors** have options for mirroring selected UV vertices. They have three options. First is Copy Mirrored UV Coords, which allows you to copy mirror UV coordinates on the X-axis based on a mirrored mesh, X-Axis, and Y-axis which allow you to mirror selected items around one or more axes. **Snap** provides you choices for snapping. We have six choices here: Selected to Pixels, Selected to Cursor, Selected to Cursor (offset), Selected to Adjacent Unselected, Cursor to Pixels, and Cursor to Selected. **Snap to Pixels** helps you snap to the nearest pixel data. We have three options for this one: Disabled, Corner, and Center.

Many of the commands in the header menu are like those tools that we already have discussed, like in the toolbar, etc. So, we don't need to memorize everything, do we? What we need is just to be familiar with everything.

Before I end up the part of UV workspace and proceed to the texture workspace, let me discuss one more thing – and those are the UDIM features of Blender.

UDIM in Blender

What is UDIM? UDIM stands for U DIMinesion, which is based on a tile system where each tile is a different texture in the overall UDIM texture array. Basically, each tile consists of its own UV space and has its own image assigned to that tile. Tiles are managed in the UDIM tiles panel where they can have a generated image assigned to them. Generally, you create several textures of different resolutions, like, for example, you have a 4k resolution texture for the major details and 2k or 1k textures for less-important details. This are helpful in big projects, and it can help you speed up the texturing process.

In the default view of the UV editor, you cannot see many of the features of the UDIM except one in the sidebar region as you can see in Figure 3-43.

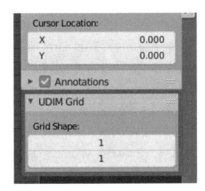

Figure 3-43. *UDIM Grid setting in Sidebar region*

If we set the numbers of the grid shape to 3:2, the effect will be like what you can see in Figure 3-44.

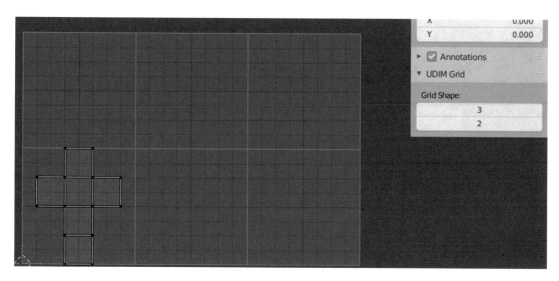

Figure 3-44. *UDIM Grid*

But that is not exactly how UDIM works. Still, my UV layout is in one tile located in the bottom left part of the image area. So, what do we need to do?

First, we need to click New ➤ set the Generated type to Color Grid and click the Tiled. The outcome should be like that shown in Figure 3-45.

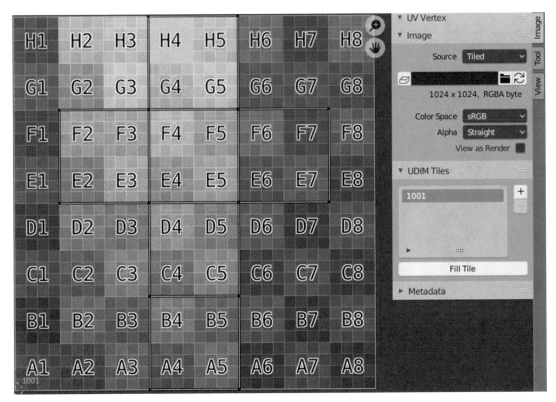

Figure 3-45. *UDIM Tiles*

You can see in our sidebar region that we have new settings, such as the panel for UDIM tiles. Let's now try to add new tiles.

Take a look at Figure 3-46 to see the effect of the new added tile.

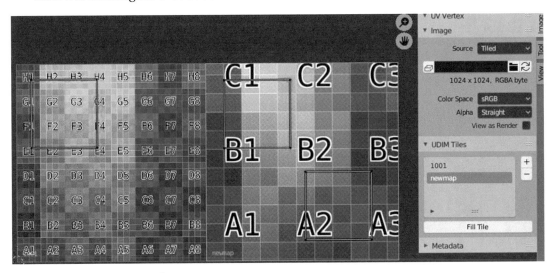

Figure 3-46. *UDIM Tiles*

I added a new tile with a label newmap that you can see at the leftmost bottom of the tile. I also set the image size to 340 x 340 pixel for you to see the difference of the high pixel tile to the lower one, and also for you to actually see one of the purposes of the UDIM. I separated the UV island of the cube and put some in the 340 x 340 pixel and some in the high pixel tile. Let's take a look its effect with a textured mesh in Figure 3-47.

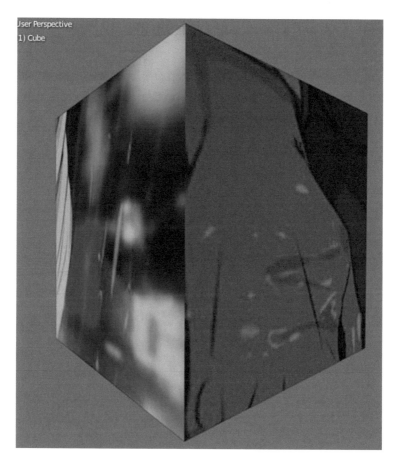

Figure 3-47. *Effect on the Textured cube*

You can see that there are differences in quality between the right side and the left side of the cube. The UV island of the face that is on the right side of the cube is in the 340 x 340 pixel, while the UV island of the face that is on the left side of the cube is in the 1024 x 1024 pixel. You can see its effect on the quality of the texture, but this canned feature of UDIM can help too in some cases. For instance, there are parts of your game assets that needed to have detailed texture, but some parts of it that don't. You can use this kind of UV mapping and texturing process to make things easier not only for you but also for the future user of your game assets.

Note   If you want to create a multiple UV map, which is also helpful in big projects, you can do this in the Properties ➤ Object Data ➤ UV maps panel, and just click the plus button to add a UV map and minus button to delete an existing map.

So now we're finally done with the UV workspace. The next chapter will cover the texture paint workspace and contains a sample project where you can use your UV workspace and texture paint workspace skills together.

CHAPTER 4

Texture It!

Good day, dear readers! Are you still having fun? Now we're in Chapter 4 of the book. Here we'll create our own textures to apply to 3D objects in the game environment. This chapter will finish with a sample project, where you can combine your skills from Chapter 3 with the skills you learn in this chapter.

Texture Paint Workspace

This is where you can create your own texture using Blender brushes and, if you have one, a graphic tablet. Take a look at Figure 4-1 to catch a glimpse of the default layout of our workspace.

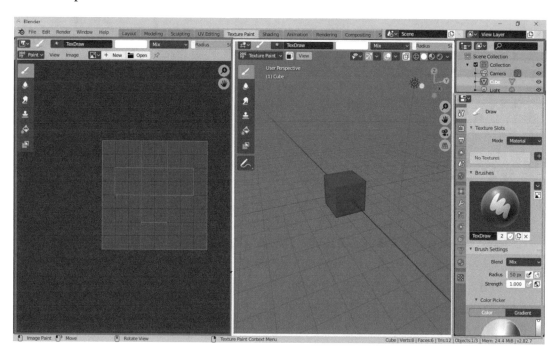

Figure 4-1. *Texture Paint Workspace (Red: Image Editor, Yellow: 3D viewport, Blue: Outliner, Orange: Properties)*

© Ezra Thess Mendoza Guevarra 2020
E. T. Mendoza Guevarra, *Creating Game Environments in Blender 3D*,
https://doi.org/10.1007/978-1-4842-6174-3_4

As you can see in Figure 4-1, we have image editor on the leftmost side, the 3D viewport in the middle, outliner in the top rightmost side, and properties in the bottom rightmost side. You can also notice that our 3D viewport here is in texture paint mode and our properties also have different kind of settings. Because of that, we have a lot of things to discuss here. First, we will start with our 3D viewport.

3D Viewport in Texture Paint Workspace

Once again, our 3D viewport here is in texture paint mode. Let's take a closer look into this mode of 3D viewport in Figure 4-2.

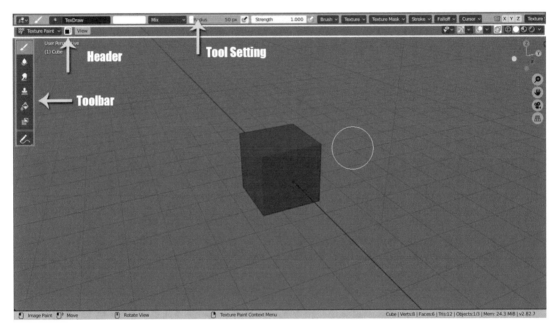

Figure 4-2. *3D viewport in Texture Paint Mode (Toggle Maximize)*

I already used toggle maximize here in order for me to show the whole editor since just dragging the border will not help to show all the tools/commands in its header. What we see in the header of 3D viewport here are just the common commands, so we will just be focusing on the toolbar and the tool settings. The settings that you can see in the tool settings, as well as in the properties, are related to the current active tool in your toolbar. This means, it will change depending on the tool you are currently using.

So, let's get started!

The tools that we have in the toolbar are Draw, Soften, Smear, Clone, Fill, Mask, and Annotate. Let's take a look at Figure 4-3 so we can have a closer look at settings related to our tools.

Figure 4-3. *Tools settings*

As you can see in Figure 4-3, draw and fill have the same settings. Actually, all of the tools from draw and mask have almost all the same settings; draw and fill have only a color picker and blending mode. Another thing you notice is that annotate has fewer settings. Note that this tool is only for leaving notes.

Let's have a brief discussion of our tools.

Draw tool is for normal brushing; **soften tool** uses a blur effect to soften or sharpen an image; **smear** takes the colors under the cursor and blends them in the direction you move the mouse; and **clone** copies the colors from the specified image, and you can do this by pressing Ctrl + left mouse button to create your source or reference to clone to. **Fill** is used to fill large areas of the image with the brush color and **mask** maps an image to the mesh and uses image intensity to mask out certain parts of the mesh during painting.

Since we almost have the same settings for each tool, let's discuss this by settings, not by tools. First stop is the **search box**. This search box has the icon that you can see in Figure 4-4 next to its brush name.

Figure 4-4. *Search box and Brush name*

When you click it, you can see a list of Blender brushes available for the tool you are currently using. By default, you only have one, but you can download some Blender brushes online from Blenderkit add-ons, etc. These settings are available in all texture paint tools **except** in annotate tools.

Next, we have the **color picker**, which is available only to the draw tool and fill tool. This allows you to choose your own color. You can choose color directly from the wheel or by getting the RGB value, HSV value, or HEX value. Since the color picker also has the eyedropper tool, you can use this to pick a color outside the color picker either from the picture imported in the Blender, from the available textures in your current project, or from the Blender UI itself.

Next stop is the **blending mode**, which is by default set to mix. This tool is only available in the draw tool and fill tool since those two are the only tools that have the color picker. I love this part since this makes me feel I'm using 2D software for digital painting. This blending mode helps you create different effects for your colors or texture. We have 24 options available for our Blending mode, which are Mix, Darken, Multiply, Color Burn, Linear Burn, Lighten, Screen, Color Dodge, Add, Overlay, Soft Light, Hard Light, Vivid Light, Linear Light, Pin Light, Difference, Exclusion, Subtract, Hue, Saturation, Color, Value, Erase Alpha, and Add Alpha. These blending modes are similar to what you can see in software like GIMP and Photoshop.

So now, let's discuss each type of blending mode.

Blending Mode

The concept of the blending mode in Blender is the same as to 2D software. The only difference is that instead of painting in canvas, you are painting in a 3D mesh. I'd like to note that the effect of some of these blending modes in the base color of the mesh isn't easy to notice, whether it was a material base color or a single texture image. Are you confused by this? Okay. Let's make this clear by looking at Figure 4-5.

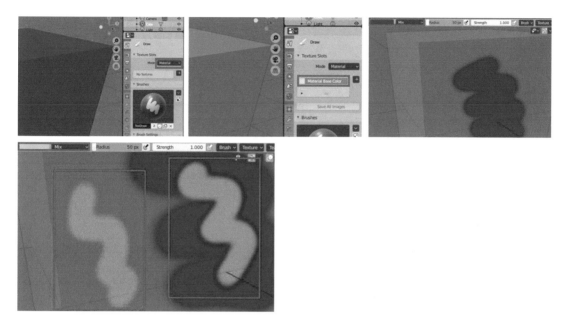

Figure 4-5. *Blending mode works with Mesh Base color using Mix Blend mode*

In Figure 4-5, notice that I applied the material base color. As I paint the color blue with the mix blending mode, you can't see its effect at a glance. But when I apply a second color, which is the green color in the place where the blue color is, you can see an effect around the green color compared to the other one that is directly painted on the mesh. This is what I mean by the effects of some blending modes aren't very visible in the base color of the mesh.

Now, one aspect is already clear. Let's proceed in discussing some basics of the blending mode. When you are using 2D software, we have three things to consider when working with blending modes: Base color, Blend Color, and Result color. Base color is the original color of the image, blend color is the color applied with the painting tool to the base layer, and the result color is the color resulting from the blend. In Blender, we have the same concept but we just need to modify some things since we don't have layers here.

For our base color, it would be the base color of the mesh object, but for us to have clearer vision in our examples, we would also assume that the first color we use to paint in the mesh is also our base color because most of the blend mode doesn't easily show its effect by just using the base mesh color. The blend colors are the colors we will choose to paint in the mesh. (Colors?) Yes. Since we are dealing with 3D painting and texturing, of course we will have more than two colors to blend. Our result color will still be the same, the output color after all the painting we've done.

So, let's start discussing each of the blending modes. First, we'll talk about the mix blend mode.

Mix Blend Mode

The **mix blend mode** is like the normal mode in Photoshop. It only does the normal texture blending mode in Blender, but if our base color and our blend color have quite large differences in values, it gives quite an effect that you can notice in the sides of the blend color.

Take a look at Figure 4-6 to see how mix blend mode works.

Figure 4-6. *Mix Blending mode works*

You can notice that in Figure 4-6, mix blend mode is like the normal mode in Photoshop. But you can see that in its edges, they have the soft blur effect that depends on the color or saturation, then turns into a burn effect.

Before we move on to our next blend mode, the blending mode in general has some categories. One of them is darken. Those blend modes under this category will turn its result color darker. In this blending mode, if you paint a white color, or any lighter color than the base color, it will become invisible or rather you will not see it applied, and anything that is darker than white, or darker than the base color, is going to have some darkening effect.

Now that we have it, let's proceed to our next blending mode, which is one of the darken blend modes, darken.

Darken Blend Mode

The **darken blend mode** looks at the luminance value in each of the RGB channels and selects either the base color or blend color depending on which is darker. Let's take a look at Figure 4-7 to see how this blend mode works.

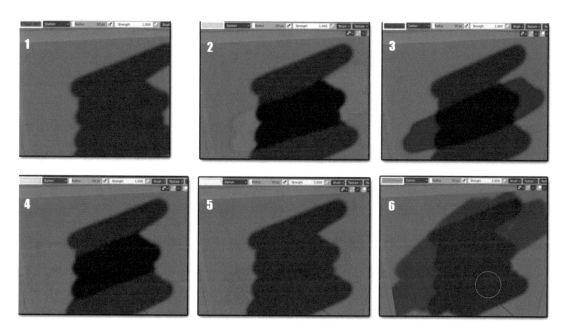

Figure 4-7. *Darken Blending mode works*

Our base color used in Figure 4-7 is the color red. You can see in different images how darken blend mode works. You can see in that when we use the green, blue, and light blue colors as our blend color, we have a darker color as a result color, while when we use the pink and peach color that are lighter than red, we didn't see any effect. This proves that any color that is lighter than the base color will not have any effect on our base color and will only affect the background of the base color, while any color that is darker than our base color will affect both the outside and the inside of the base color.

Okay. This might get a little confusing because of many technical things. For both darken and multiply, these are the rules applied: when the blend color is lighter than the base color, it will become invisible. If the blend color is also a color white, it will also become invisible. When the blend color is darker than the base color, you will see a result color. If the blend color is darker than the color white, you will see a result color. This also be applied in the next two-blend mode, which is color burn and linear burn, but of course, there are also some differences in effects.

Let's now proceed to multiply blend mode, which is also part of the darken blend mode.

Multiply Blend Mode

Multiply blend mode multiplies the luminosity of the base color by the blend color. The output color or the resulting color is always a darker color. White produces no change while black pixels remain.

Let's take a look at Figure 4-8 to see how this blend mode works.

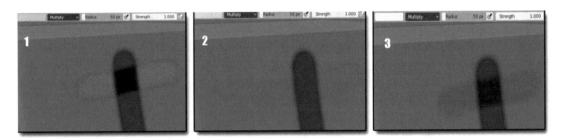

Figure 4-8. *Multiply Blending mode works*

You see that its effect is the same as in the darken blend mode. Their difference lies in how they calculate the luminosity of the colors, but their rules between the darker and lighter colors are the same. As you can see in Figure 4-8, the color green, which is darker than the color blue, results in a darker color. The light blue blend color doesn't have an effect on our base color since it is lighter than our base color; and last, the peach color has a minimal effect on our base color since it is a little darker than white.

If that is already clear, let's now proceed to our next blend mode, which is the color burn.

Color Burn Blend Mode

Color burn blend mode is part of the category of darken blend modes that gives you a darker result than Multiply by increasing the contrast between the base and the blend colors, resulting in more highly saturated midtones and reduced highlights.

Take a look at Figure 4-9 to see how color burn works.

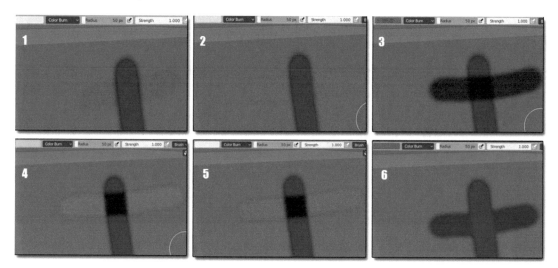

Figure 4-9. *Color Burn Blending mode works*

You can see in image Figure 4-9 that in these blending modes, lighter colors don't affect the base color while the darker colors have an impact. Unlike in multiply and darken, there are some instances where lighter colors can affect the base color: for example, it is darker than white and isn't lighter than the base color. Here in color burn, as long as it is lighter than the base color, it will not affect the base color.

Next stop is the linear burn blend mode.

Linear Burn Blend Mode

Linear burn blend mode is part of the category of darken blend modes that decreases the brightness of the base color based on the value of blend colors. The result is darker than multiply but less saturated than color burn. Linear burn also produces the most contrast to darker colors than any of the other blending modes in the darker group. Let's take a look at how linear burn works in Figure 4-10.

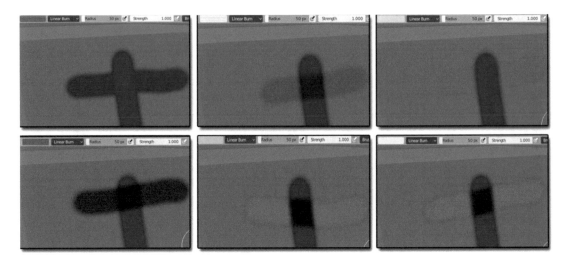

Figure 4-10. *Linear Burn Blending mode works*

Its result color is the same as Color Burn at first glance, but if you look at it closely, you will see the real effect of the Linear Burn. At some point, it is darker than the Darker Blend mode, Multiply Blend Mode, and Color Burn Blend mode.

Okay. We will have now the blending modes, which are the opposite of the darken blend modes, the **lighten blend modes**. These modes will turn result colors to brighter colors. When you paint black, it will become invisible and anything that is brighter than black is going to have some darkening effect.

Now, let's start with the lighten blend mode.

Lighten Blend Mode

Lighten blend mode takes a look at the base color and blend colors, and it keeps whichever one of the two is the lightest. If the blend colors and the base colors are the same, then no change is applied. Lighten looks at the three RGB channels separately when blending the pixels.

Let's take a look at Figure 4-11 to see how this blend mode works.

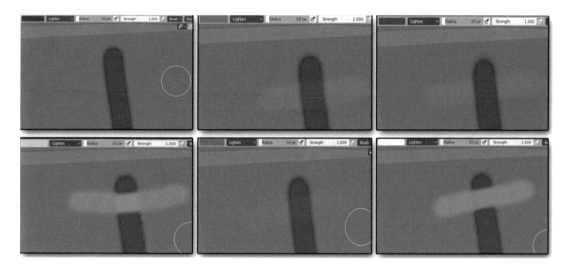

Figure 4-11. *Lighten Blending mode works*

You can notice that the dark blue doesn't have an effect at all – like it's invisible. You can't see anything. When I applied the blue color, it only affected the mesh or the outside of the base color. When I chose white as my blend color, you notice that it looks like a solid color when I paint it across our base color unlike the others, which look like a highlighter color. You see in this mode that the lighter the blend color is, the more visible the result color will be.

Now, let's proceed to our next lighten blend mode, which is the screen blend mode.

Screen Blend Mode

Screen blend mode is where the resulting color is always a brighter color. It can produce many different levels of brightening depending on luminosity values of the blend colors.

Let's take a look at Figure 4-12 to see how this mode works.

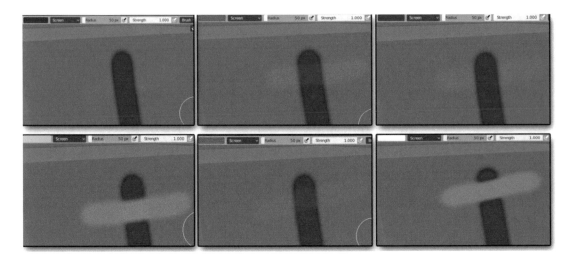

Figure 4-12. *Screen Blending mode works*

Unlike in lighten blend mode, that part of the dark blue at least has a bit of effect here, though it isn't that visible, but still for the other five colors, pink, blue (which is the same as the base color), green, red, and white, it is the same as the lighten.

Let's move on to the other lighten blend mode, which is the color dodge.

Color Dodge Blend Mode

Color dodge blend mode gives you a brighter effect than screen blending by decreasing the contrast between the base color and the blend colors, resulting in saturated midtones and blown highlights.

Take a look at Figure 4-13 to see the effects of this mode.

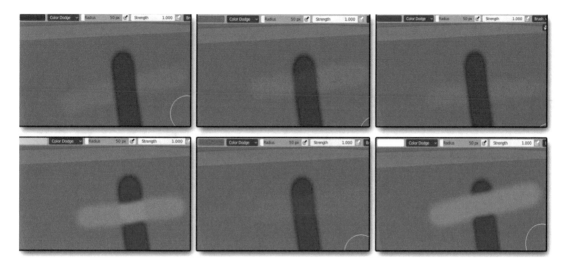

Figure 4-13. *Color Dodge Blending mode works*

Again, as you can see, the effect on the darker blue here is that it is much more visible compared to the other two, which are the screen and lighten. You can notice that their differences lie in how these lighten blend modes treat the darker colors because they have the same rule when it comes to light colors like pink, which has the same color of the base color and white color.

Now, let's proceed to the last lighten blend mode but not the last blend mode, add.

Add Blend Mode

Add blend mode produces a similar but stronger result than screen or color dodge. This blending mode looks at the color information in each channel and brightens the base color to reflect the blend color by increasing the brightness.

Let's see Figure 4-14 to see how the add blend mode works.

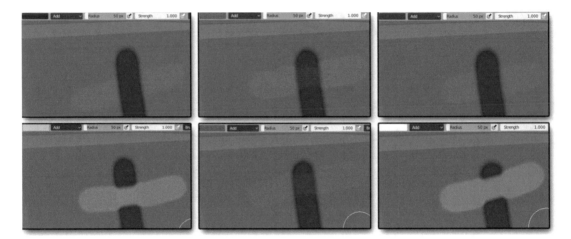

Figure 4-14. *Add Blending mode works*

You can see in Figure 4-14, though add blend mode has the same rule with the other lighten blend mode, its impact is still different. Its result looks more visible than the other three.

So, we're done with the lighten blend mode. We'll now proceed to another set of blend modes, which are called contrast blending modes. In this kind of mode, the rule was if you paint a color with 50% gray with this mode, it will become invisible. This mode creates contrast by both lightening and darkening the result colors by using complementary blending modes to create the blend.

Now that we already know how it works, let's start the discussion of each blending mode under this category.

Overlay Blend Mode

First stop is the **overlay blend mode**. This mode is a combination of multiply and screen with the base color always shining through. Overlay uses the screen at half strength on colors lighter than 50% gray while it uses multiply at half strength on colors darker than 50% gray.

Another way of thinking about overlay is by thinking of shifting midtones. Dark blend colors shift the midtones to darker colors, and light tones shift the midtones to brighter colors.

Let's take a look at Figure 4-15 to see how this blending mode works.

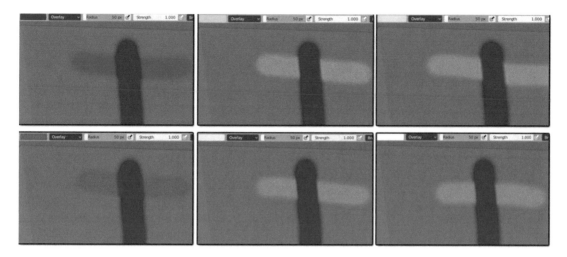

Figure 4-15. *Overlay Blending mode works*

Notice something at the sides of the color blue? There is some effect in the part where we paint with the overlay blend mode. It seems that the effect doesn't only in the color that can be seen, but also these blending mode create a texture like effect that can be seen in the sides of the color stroke.

Now, let's proceed to our next contrast blending mode, which is soft light.

Soft Light Blend Mode

Soft light blend mode is very much like overlay. It applies either a darkening or lightening effect depending on the luminance values, but in a much more subtle way. You can think of soft light as a softer version of overlay without the harsh contrast.

Take a look at Figure 4-16 to see how soft light works.

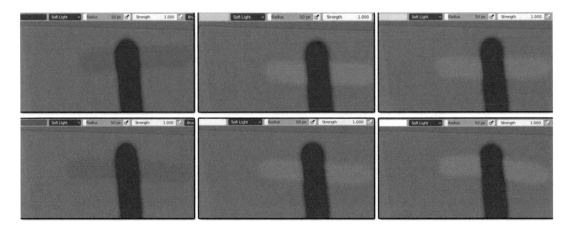

Figure 4-16. *Soft Light Blending mode works*

In our example in Figure 4-16, we see more of a lightening effect in soft light blend mode, though we can see some darkening in part of the white color. Well, as I stated above, it applies lightening or darkening depending on the luminance values of the colors.

Hard Light Blend Mode

At the next stop, we have the **hard light blend mode**, which combines the multiply and screen blending modes using the brightness values of the blend colors to make its calculations. The results with hard light tend to be intense. It sounds like it would have something in common with soft light, but it does not. It is more closely related to overlay.

Take a look at Figure 4-17 to see how this blend mode works.

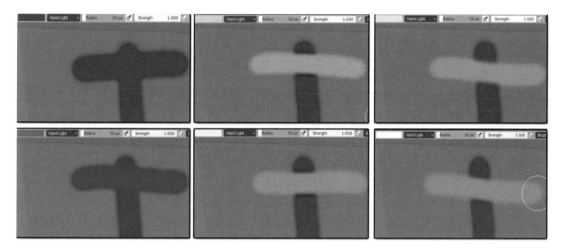

Figure 4-17. *Hard Light Blending mode works*

If you look at Figure 4-17, you can see that our result colors look more like the result color for mix blend mode except that you don't see any burn-like effect on the sides in any of our result color examples. This might be the reason why the resulting colors of hard light tend to be intense.

So, let's now proceed with our next contrast blend mode, which is vivid light.

Vivid Light Blend Mode

Vivid light blend mode is like an extreme version of overlay and soft light. Anything darker than 50% gray is darkened, and anything lighter than 50% gray is lightened.

Let's take a look at Figure 4-18 to see how this blend mode works.

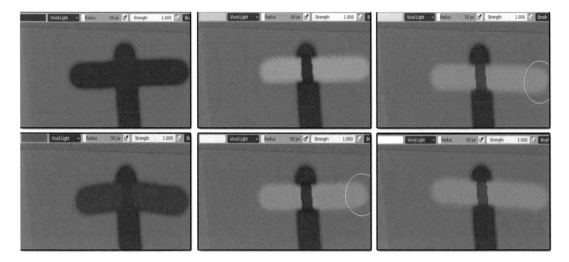

Figure 4-18. *Vivid Light Blending mode works*

Here, we can see a visible texture effect in the middle of the blue color. But wait, you can only see the effect of vivid light using a color either lighter or darker than the base color, but you cannot see its effect if you use a blend color with the same color of the base color, unlike soft light and overlay. You can also see that its color is as intense as hard light here.

So, now, let's proceed to the linear light blend mode.

Linear Light Blend Mode

Linear light blend mode uses a combination of the add blending mode on lighter pixels and a linear burn on darker pixels.

Take a look at Figure 4-19 to see how this blend mode works.

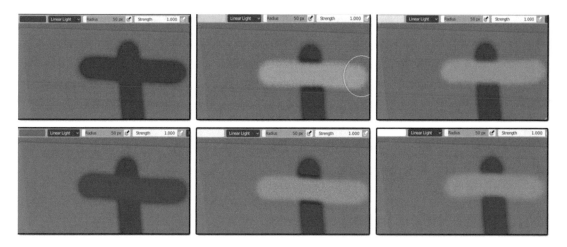

Figure 4-19. *Linear Light Blending mode works*

In our result color in Figure 4-19, linear light has the same effect as hard light. They have the same intensities, and you can't easily see their difference.

Now, let's proceed to the last contrast mode we have here, pin light.

Pin Light Blend Mode

Pin light blend mode is an extreme blending mode that performs a darken and lighten blending mode simultaneously. It can result in patches or blotches, and it completely removes all midtones.

Take a look at Figure 4-20 to see how this blend mode works.

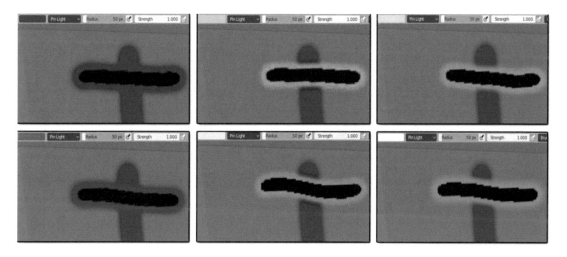

Figure 4-20. *Pin Light Blending mode works*

It's very clear and visible in Figure 4-20. The effect, or should we say, the texture-like effect, which might be the blotches or patches of pin light. It's very clear to see the difference of this mode to other contrast blend modes.

Let's discuss the last category of blending mode that we will have here, inversion blending modes. This mode looks for variations between the base and blend colors to create the blend.

Now that it was already given, let's start discussing the blend mode that is under this category. Let's start with the difference.

Difference Blend Mode

Difference blend mode uses the difference of the base color and blend pixels as the resulting color. White color inverts the base color while black produces no change. Dark gray colors apply a slight darkening effect.

Let's take a look at Figure 4-21 to see how this blend mode works.

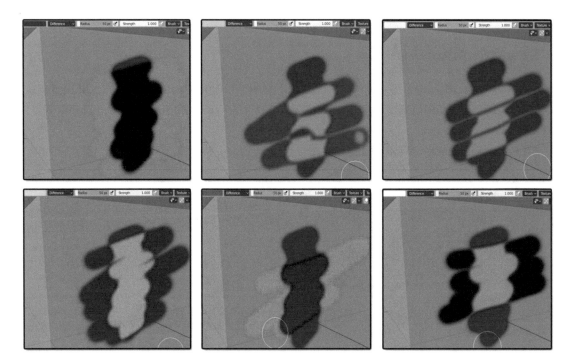

Figure 4-21. *Difference Blending mode works*

Remember that our base color is the mesh base color, and we are only using the blue color for us to have a clearer vision of what's going on with our blend modes. See that when we use the color blue, it turns a resulting color of yellow and turns the blue color painted in the mesh to black. The green color results in pink and turns the blue color to light blue. The yellow color results in the blue color and turns the blue color to white. The light blue color results in red and turns the blue color to green. The pink color results in green and turns the blue color to red. Last, the white color results in black and turns the blue color to yellow. This is the example of how this blend mode uses the differences of the base color and blend colors.

Let's now proceed to our next inversion blend mode, which is exclusion.

Exclusion Blend Mode

Exclusion blend mode is very similar to difference. Blending with white inverts the base color values, while blending with black produces no change. However, blending with 50% gray produces 50% gray.

Take a look at Figure 4-22 to see how the exclusion blend mode works.

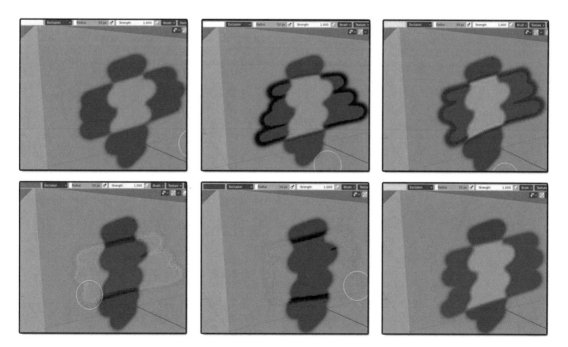

Figure 4-22. *Exclusion Blending mode works*

As you can see in Figure 4-22, exclusion has a different kind of effect more than the effect on its color. For example, in the part where I used the color pink as a blend color together with the blue, it results in a light blue color with a green stroke effect on the outside while a red stroke plus a pink fill in the part that hit the blue color results. This effect also shows in the part where I used the color white, light blue, and blue. This didn't show when I used the color green and yellow, but in the part of color yellow, the part that hit the color blue looks like it has been erased.

You can see here that this blend mode has an interesting effect that is worth learning.

Now, let's proceed to our last contrast blending mode, but not the last blend mode to discuss, which is the Subtract Blend Mode.

Subtract Blend Mode

Subtract blend mode subtracts pixel values from the base color. This blending mode drastically darkens pixels by subtracting brightness. Black has no effect. Only as the blend values get brighter does the result get darker.

Let's see Figure 4-23 to see subtract blend mode at work.

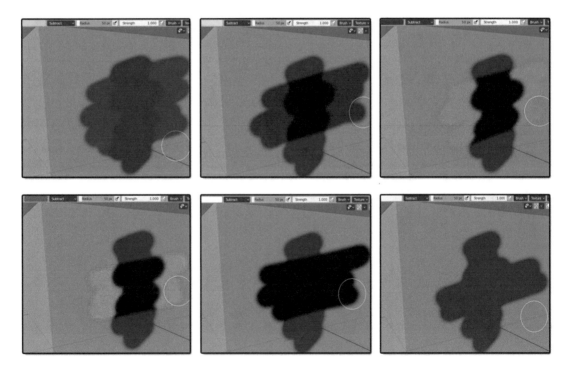

Figure 4-23. *Subtract Blending mode works*

We can see in Figure 4-23 that the result color we produce using the subtract blend mode is the opposite of the color we've chosen. It is just like white to black, green to pink, or yellow to blue.

Now, we're done with the three contrast blend modes. We still have six blend modes to discuss: Hue, Saturation, Color, Value, Erase Alpha, and Add Alpha. Let's keep going!

Hue Blend Mode

Hue blend mode preserves the luminosity and saturation of the base color while adopting the hue of the blend color.

Let's take a look at Figure 4-24 to see how this blend mode works.

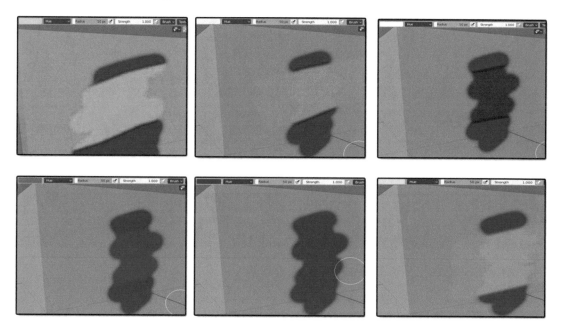

Figure 4-24. *Hue Blending mode works*

As you can see in Figure 4-24, it seems this blend mode doesn't have any effect on base mesh color but if you look closely on the part where I used the light blue, white, and yellow colors, it does have an effect but it's not that visible. But also, you can notice how white turns to red rather than another white. This is because there is no white in a hue or black. It is only RGB. Hue is like turning the color wheel so it changes colors but doesn't change the saturation. The saturation is like moving from the center to the edge of the color wheel, and the value is adjusting the slider on the side of the color wheel, making everything darker or lighter.

Now, let's move on to our next blend mode, which is saturation.

Saturation Blend Mode

Saturation blend mode preserves the luminosity and hue of the base color while adopting the saturation of the blend colors. A black-and-white blend color also turns the image into grayscale because the base color doesn't have saturation.

Take a look at Figure 4-25 to see how saturation works.

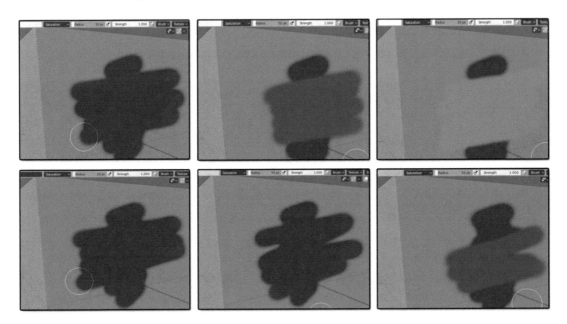

Figure 4-25. *Saturation Blending mode works*

Quite an effect, right? Here, we can say that when you choose a pure hue as a blend color, we can only get an effect the same as you can see in the two images placed on the left side of Figure 4-25, where I used blue and yellow as blend colors. You see that it has a result color where we have a blue color and a pink color mix in on the sides. But as we choose a color where its saturation value is lesser for the blend color, the result output has a slight change too. It became lighter, as you can see in our example. However, when we use white as a blend color, we cannot see any effect at all. Again, this happens because I'm just using the hue, or the RGB, value without using the saturation value in it; but unless you change the saturation of the color to differe from the saturation of the first color you use, you will see some big differences.

Now, let's take a look in our next blend mode, which is color.

Color Blend Mode

Color blend mode preserves the luminosity of the base color while adopting the hue and saturation of the blend color.

Take a look at Figure 4-26 to see how this mode works.

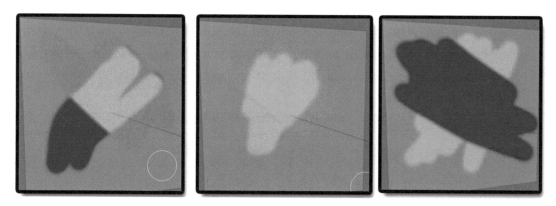

Figure 4-26. *Color Blending mode works*

As you can see in Figure 4-26, this blend mode has an effect of a highlighter. Well, depending on the combination of saturation of colors you use, it also determines the effect you will have in your output.

Let's now proceed to our next blend mode, which is value.

Value Blend Mode

Value blend mode preserves the luminosity of the base color while adopting the value of the blend colors.

Take a look at Figure 4-27 to see how the value blend mode works.

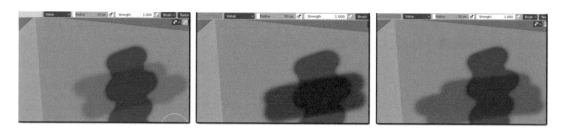

Figure 4-27. *Value Blending mode works*

As you can see in Figure 4-27, most of the result colors from this blend mode are close to a gray color.

Now let's have these two special blend modes, which are erase alpha and add alpha.

Erase Alpha and Add Alpha Blend Modes

Erase alpha and **add alpha** are different from the rest because their effects aren't about the color. Its more about the textures. When you use erase alpha, it erases or makes the texture invisible while when you use add alpha, it adds or brings back what's been erased or hidden with erase alpha.

Take a look at Figure 4-28 to see how these two-blend modes work.

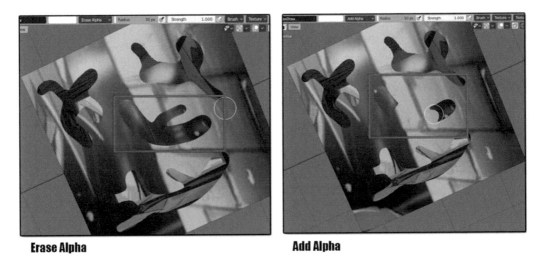

Erase Alpha   **Add Alpha**

Figure 4-28. *Erase and Add alpha Blending modes work*

Its already clear in Figure 4-28 how erase alpha makes the texture invisible while add alpha makes the texture visible again.

Before we end our topic with the blending modes, let's have another example for some of our blending modes and see it in Figure 4-29.

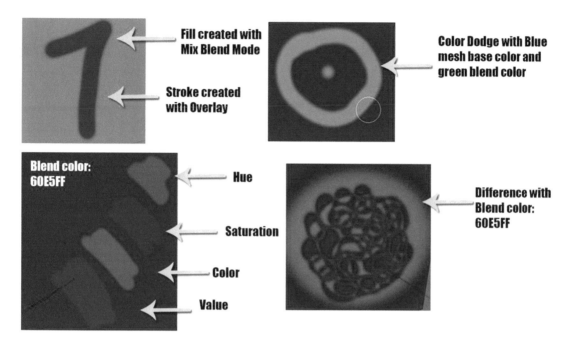

Figure 4-29. *Some examples of how Blending Mode works*

Now we're done with the blending modes. We will be going back to the settings that can be found in the header.

Tool Settings

Let's now proceed to the one tool next to the blending mode and that is the radius.

Radius settings simply refer to the size of the brush of your tools. This setting is available in all texture paint workspace tools except in annotate tools. Beside the radius is an icon with an image of a small pen. This is for enabling brush sensitivity in size when using a graphic tablet. Next, we have **strength**, which is for indicating how powerful the effect of the brush is when applied. Beside strength is also an icon with an image of a small pen. This is for enabling brush sensitivity for strength when using a graphic tablet.

Brush

Next to strength are drop-down advance settings for brush. Though all of the tools have these settings, except annotate, they have different options available for this part. See Figure 4-30 to see options available for these settings in each tool.

Figure 4-30. *Advance Brush settings*

- For the draw and clone tool, we have two options: **accumulate**, which allows a stroke to accumulate on itself when enabled; and **affect alpha**, which allows changes to the alpha channel while painting when enabled.

- For the smear and fill tool, we only have affect alpha.

- For the mask tool, we have both affect alpha; accumulate; and another one, which is **mask value**, for indicating the vertex weight when the brush is applied.

- For the soften tool, aside from affect alpha, we have **direction**, which indicates the direction of your brush. We have two options here: soften and sharp. Soften is used to paint a blur effect while sharpen enhances the contrast of the image as you paint it over. **Sharp threshold** indicates the threshold value limit of where the sharpening will be applied. **Blur mode** controls how neighboring pixels are weighted when calculating that difference.

Texture

Next to our advanced brush settings are other drop-down settings; one is texture as you can see in Figure 4-31.

Figure 4-31. *Texture settings*

This time, this is the same for all tools (Draw, Soften, Smear, Fill, Clone, and Mask). **New** means of course creating a new texture to be used as a color source. **Mapping** sets the way the texture is applied to the brush stroke. Mapping has five options: View Plane, Tiled, 3D, Random, and Stencil.

- **View Plane:** the current view angle is used to project brush texture onto the model.

- **Tiled:** It will tile the texture across the screen so moving the brush appears to move separately from the texture.

- **3D** allows the brush to take full advantage of procedural textures.

- **Random** picks random texture coordinates from each dab.

- **Stencil** works by projecting the paint from the viewport space on the mesh canvas.

We also have settings for **angle**, which set the rotation angle of the brush; **offset** which offsets the texture map placement in the X-, Y-, and Z-axes; and **size**, which sets the scale of the texture in each axis.

Texture Mask

Let's proceed to our next setting, which is the texture mask. Just like texture, this setting is the same for our six tools. Let's take a look at Figure 4-32 to see what we have here.

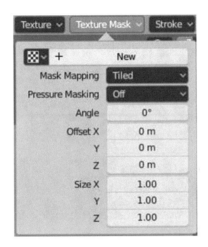

Figure 4-32. *Texture Mask settings*

So, the settings that we have for texture mask are almost the same as what we have for texture settings except the part of pressure masking. So, let's just discuss this part.

Pressure masking allows us to clip the mask result based on pressure, creating areas of no paint when low pressure is applied to the brush. It has three options: Off, Ramp, and Cutoff. **Off** means deactivating the pressure masking. **Ramp** means distributing the mask effect above the pressure value, and **cutoff** means simply to select between zero and one based on the stylus pressure.

Stroke

Let's now have our next setting, which is the stroke setting. The options for this setting are also the same for Draw, Soften, Fill, Smear, Mask, and Clone tools. Let's now see Figure 4-33 to see the available options for this setting.

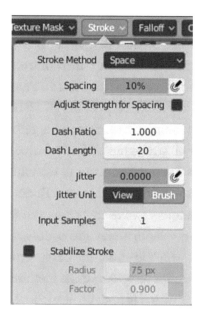

Figure 4-33. *Stroke settings*

So, what we have here is the **stroke method,** which defines the way brush strokes are applied in the canvas. We have seven options for this:

- **Dots** apply paint on each mouse move step.

- **Drag Dots** leave only one dab on the canvas, which can be placed by dragging.

- **Space** creates brush strokes as a series of dots.

- **Airbrush:** the flow of the brush continues as long as the mouse click is held.

- **Anchored** creates a single dab at the brush location.

- **Line** lets you define a line in a screen space by clicking and dragging.

- **Curve** defines a curve in a screen space.

Spacing represents the percentage of the brush radius. This is only available under the Space, Line, and Curve Stroke methods. **Adjust strength for spacing** attenuates the brush strength according to spacing. It is only available under the Space, Line, and Curve stroke methods. **Dash ratio** is the ratio of samples in a cycle that the brush is enabled. This is only available under the pace stroke method. **Dash length** is the length of a dash cycle measured in stroke samples. This is also only available in space stroke methods.

Jitter jitters the position of the brush while painting. This option is available under all stroke methods. The pen-like icon next to Jitter is for enabling brush sensitivity for Jitter when using your graphic tablet. **Jitter unit** controls how the brush Jitter is measured. We have two options here: View and Brush. These options are also available under all stroke methods. Next, we have **input samples** where the recent mouse locations, which are the input samples, are averaged together to smooth brush strokes. This option is available under all stroke methods. **Stabilize stroke** makes the stroke lag behind the cursor and applies a smoothed curve to the path of the cursor when enabled. There are two settings under this option: Radius and Factor. **Radius** sets the minimum distance from the last point before a stroke continues and **factor** sets the amount of smoothing. Stabilize stroke is available under space, dots, and airbrush stroke methods.

We also have **draw curve**, which is under the curve stroke method. It executes the curved stroke. **Rate**, which is under airbrush stroke method sets interval between paints for airbrush, and **edge to edge**, which is under the anchored stroke method, determines the brush location and orientation by a two-point circle where the first click is one point and dragging places the second point opposite from the first.

Falloff

Now that we're done with the stroke setting, let's look at the falloff setting (Figure 4-34).

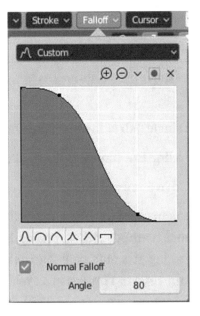

Figure 4-34. *Falloff settings*

We have ten curve presets here: Custom, Smooth, Smoother, Sphere, Root, Sharp, Linear, Sharper, Inverse Square, and Constant. By default, the mask tool is set to smooth while fill, draw, smear, soften, and clone tools are set to custom. So, at first glance, you will think they have different settings, but that's not the case.

Enabling normal falloff means as faces point away from the view, the brush strokes fade away to prevent harsh edges. Angle is the angle at which the falloff begins.

Cursor

Next to falloff settings, we have cursor settings. Take a look at Figure 4-35 to see what we have in these settings.

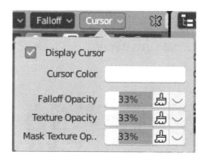

Figure 4-35. *Cursor settings*

Display cursor allows you to see the special cursor that helps you by displaying the information about the brush. **Cursor color** sets the color of the brush ring while performing a stroke. **Falloff opacity** sets the opacity for the falloff. **Texture opacity** sets the opacity for the Texture, and **mask texture opacity** sets the opacity for the texture mask.

Note   The cursor settings are the same for our Draw, Fill, Smear, Soften, Clone, and Mask tools.

Symmetry

Now, we have the **symmetry** setting, which can be found in all texture paint tools, including annotate. Take a look at Figure 4-36 to see what it looks like.

Figure 4-36. *Symmetry settings*

This setting will help you mirror what you are doing in one part of the mesh to the other side, depending on what axis you choose. It is just like the mirror modifier for our modeling.

Texture Slot

Next is the texture slot. **Texture slot** is where you add the texture or material base color for your mesh. This is the most important setting since you cannot start your project without a material base color or a texture in it. These are also available in all tools except for annotate tools.

Take a look at Figure 4-37 to see this setting.

Settings for Material   **Setting for Single Image**

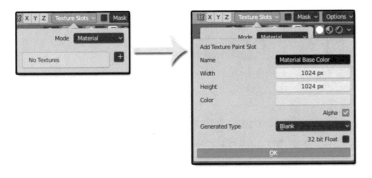

Figure 4-37. *Texture Slots settings*

First, we have **mode** where you can choose a mode of texture you want to have. We have two types of mode: Material and Single Image. **Material** mode is the one we called material base color or what is created inside Blender while the **single image** is the one that is a texture or something imported from outside Blender.

To create a material base color, first you will add one by clicking the plus icon. Whatever you choose here, the next settings will be the ones in the middle of Figure 4-37. You will be asked for a name or label for your base color, width and height for the pixel resolution of your base color, color for the main color, and generated type for what kind of image you want your material to be. For a generated type, we have three options: Blank, which generates a blank image; UV Grid, which generates a grid to test UV mappings; and Color, which generates improved UV grid test UV mappings.

For single image, we only have simple settings. New means new texture, and open means to open or browse texture. The UVMap is something related to our UV editing since this texture will directly flatten to the mesh and means Blender will also automatically create a UV map for this one. The last one is the interpolation, which has two sets of option: Linear and Closest. These two have lots of formulas to explain so I leave it with that.

Mask

Let's now proceed with the mask settings, which all texture paint tools have, including annotate tools. Take a look at Figure 4-38 to see the settings.

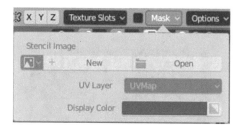

Figure 4-38. *Mask settings*

This is another setting for masking. This is for if you ever don't want to paint on some part, but you want to freely paint on the other parts of the mesh. By using this mask setting, you can cover up for that part you want to avoid, being able to paint on it and freely paint on the other parts. You can even use this to trace on an image.

Take a look at Figure 4-39 to see how this works.

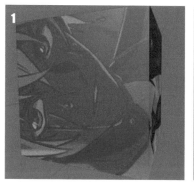
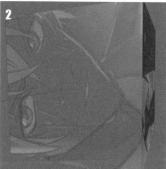
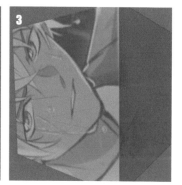

Figure 4-39. *Mask settings*

So, in image 1 of Figure 4-39, we applied the mask. In image 2, we painted over the mask using mix blend, and in image 3, you can see the result of what I did using the mask setting.

This is just one of the uses of masking.

Basically, this is how mask settings work. The new button is for saving the result of the masking you created in the Blender, like in image 3 of Figure 4-39. Open is for browsing the image for masking, UV layer again is for directing Blender so that the result of what we did in the mask setting has a UV layout created automatically, and the display color is for the color you want to use for the masking. It will affect the output so make sure to choose wisely.

Options

Let's now proceed to the options settings and take a look at Figure 4-40 to see what it has for us.

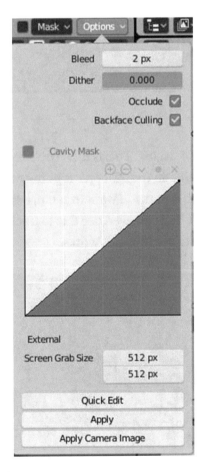

Figure 4-40. *Options settings*

So what we have here are **bleed**, which extends paint beyond the faces UVs to reduce seams; and **dither**, which is the amount of dithering when painting on byte images; **occlude**, which only paints onto the faces directly under the brush when enabled; **backface culling**, which ignores faces pointing away from the view; **cavity mask**, which masks painting according to the mesh geometry cavity; **screen grab size**, which is the size to capture the image for re-projecting; **quick edit**, which edits a snapshot of the viewport in an external image editor; **apply**, which projects an edited image back onto the object; and **apply camera image**, which projects an edited render from the active camera back onto the object.

Annotation Stroke Placement

Now, to close our discussion on tool settings, let's proceed to our last setting, which is the annotation stroke placement that can only be found in the annotate tool. Take a look at Figure 4-41 to see this setting.

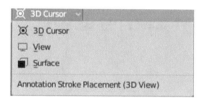

Figure 4-41. *Annotation Stroke Placement settings*

We have three options for this setting: **3D cursor** that draws strokes at the 3D cursor location, **view** that sticks strokes to the view, and **surface** that sticks strokes to the surface.

Properties

Okay. Now we're already done discussing that can be seen in the header. The next should be properties, but if we look closely at it, what we can see in the properties are almost the same as at what we can see in the header. There are only some parts that are not in the header. Let's take a look at Figure 4-42 to see the comparison of the settings in the tool settings and in the properties.

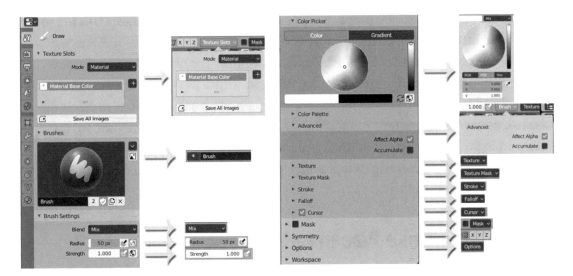

Figure 4-42. *Tool Settings compared to Properties*

See that almost all of the settings that can be found in tool settings can also be found in properties aside from the two, color palette and workspace, so let's just discuss these two so we won't leave anything behind in the settings.

Color Palette

Color palette is where you can store or create swatches for your project. This is important as a reference color so you don't need to memorize or list down the color code of the list of colors you are going to use or have already used. What you will just do is to use the eyedropper and pick it up in the color palette. This will be more convenient, making you more at ease while doing your project.

This is only available in fill and draw tools.

Workspace

Workspace has settings that can help you change your editor mode whenever you want to by selecting the editor mode in the select menu. It also has the list of the previous add-ons you already used. Take a look at Figure 4-43 to see a sample of its settings.

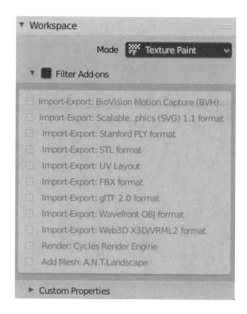

Figure 4-43. *Workspace Panel*

Now that we're already done with the tools and settings in the 3D viewport, we're going to proceed in the tools and settings that we have in the image editor.

Image Editor in Texture Paint Workspace

Image editor is another place where you can do painting for your texture. Here, your 3D mesh is in its flattened image, just like how it was in UV editing. As you do your painting, you can see your output in the 3D viewport on the right side. Our image editor is in paint mode, which is the mode applicable for texture painting.

Take a look at Figure 4-44 to catch a glimpse at the default setup of our image editor.

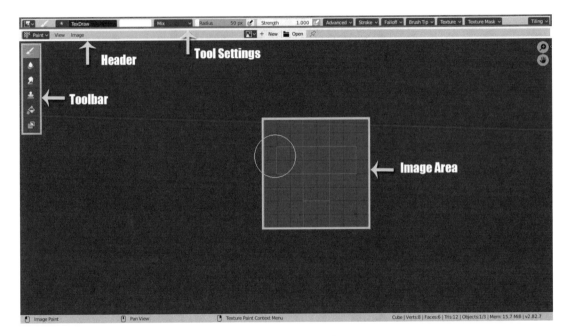

Figure 4-44. *Image Editor in Texture Paint Workspace*

I use toggle maximize (Ctrl + Spacebar) to show the whole image editor in Figure 4-44. What we have here are toolbar, tool settings, header, and image area.

Image area, just like in UV editor, is where you can paint the 2D equivalent of your mesh.

Our header only has the select menu for editor mode, view, and image menus, and new and open buttons for image or texture.

The interesting commands in the view menu are as follows (the rest are very similar to what we saw in other view menus in this book):

- **Adjust Last Operation** is for you to control if you want to disable or enable the last operation features, which helps you easily trace back what your last activity was using one tool.

- **Update Automatically** allows you to enable or disable this feature that allows you to update other affected window spaces automatically to reflect changes during interactive operations.

- **Show Metadata** allows you to enable or disable the features that display metadata properties of the image.

- **Display Texture Paint UVs** display overlays of texture paint UV layers.

- **Show Same Material** displays only faces with the currently displayed image assigned.

The image menu is the same as what we have with the UV editor menu. And yes, most of the header menus in Blender have the same commands or tools under it.

Just like in 3D viewport, our tool settings are connected to our tools so it changes depending on the tools that are currently active. Thankfully, most of the tools have the same settings. And most of them are the same settings as the ones in the 3D viewport.

So, let's get started!

Tool Settings

Take a look at Figure 4-45 to see our tools together with their tool settings.

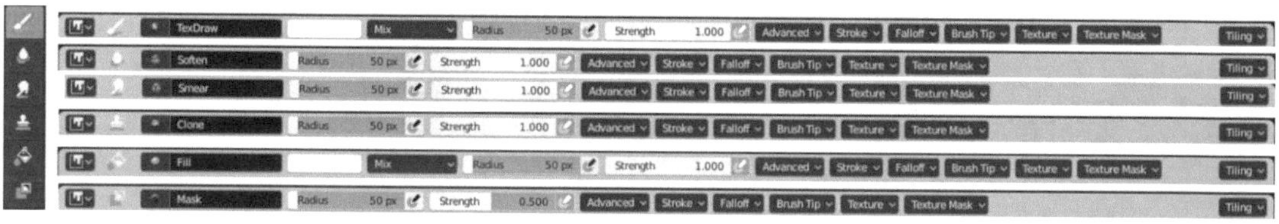

Figure 4-45. *Image editor's Toolbar and Tool settings*

We have Draw, Soften, Smear, Clone, Fill, and Mask. Unlike in 3D viewport, we don't have an annotate tool here.

As you can see in Figure 4-45, we almost have the same settings for these six tools. First, we have the **search box** where you can search brushes available in Blender; the **brush name** indicates the name of the brush/tool. We also have the **color picker** where you can pick the color of your choice for painting, which is only available for fill and draw tools. Next to it is the **blending mode** where you can choose the type of effect you want with your painting, which is by default is in mix mode and only available for fill and draw tools. We also have **radius**, which sets the size of the radius of your brush tool; and **strength**, which sets how powerful the effect of the brush is when applied.

Advanced Settings

Now we have these advanced settings that are somehow a little bit different from the ones in the 3D viewport and also vary depending on the active tools. Take a look at Figure 4-46 to see the options available under these settings for different tools.

169

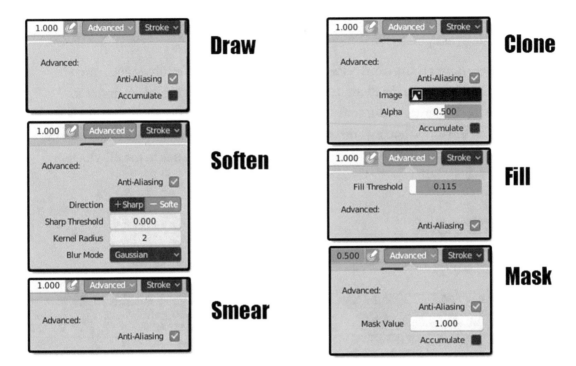

Figure 4-46. *Advanced Settings*

Our tools have common options in advanced settings. One of them is anti-aliasing, which can be found under the advance settings of all tools. **Anti-aliasing** smooths the edges of the strokes.

- Our draw tool has **accumulate** that allows a stroke to accumulate on itself when enabled and this can also be seen in the clone and mask tool.

- Mask tool has a **mask value** that is for indicating the vertex weight when a brush is applied.

- Fill tool has a **fill threshold** that is for the threshold above which filling is not propagated.

- Our Clone tool has an **image** where it can browse an image for cloning; and **alpha**, which is for the opacity of the clone image display.

- Soften tool has **direction**, which indicates the direction of your brush. We have two options here: Soften and Sharp. Soften is used to paint a blur effect while sharpen enhances the contrast of the image as you paint it over. **Sharp threshold** indicates the threshold value limit of where the sharpening will be applied. **Kernel radius**, which sets the radius of kernel, is used for softening and sharpening in pixels. **Blur mode** controls how neighboring pixels are weighted when calculating that difference.

Note   Stroke setting is the same as what we have in the 3D viewport.

Brush Tip

Now, let's proceed to another setting that is called Brush tip. Take a look at Figure 4-47 to see this setting.

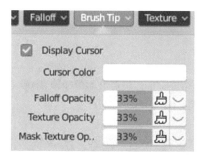

Figure 4-47. *Brush Tip Settings*

(Wait a minute. It seems I already saw these settings before. Ah! In cursor settings in 3D viewport!) Yes. The cursor settings in the 3D viewport are called brush tips in the image editor, but still they have the same function.

Note   Texture and texture mask settings are the same as what we have in the 3D viewport.

Tiling

Now, we're down to the last setting we have in the image editor for all the tools, which is tiling. Take a look at Figure 4-48 to see what these settings have.

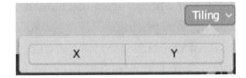

Figure 4-48. *Tiling Settings*

So simple right? It's because its purpose was for helping you create tiling for your textures, either in the X-axis or Y-axis.

We're already discussed the image editor. Since its settings are almost the same as what we have in the 3D viewport, we don't need to discuss it in depth.

We already know that the texture paint workspace, or Blender itself, gives us two ways to paint our texture. We can do it in 3D way (in 3D viewport) or in 2D way (image editor). The tools are the same, so it's a matter of when's its convenient and when we want to be creative. Let's begin our sample project!

Sample Project

We're now going to put some texturing in our sample project. Let's once again take a look at what we have modeled in Figure 4-49.

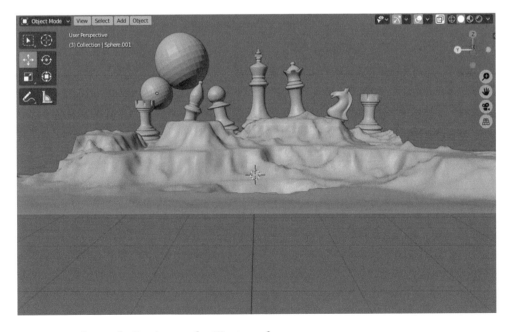

Figure 4-49. *Sample Project to be Textured*

Before we have our game assets textured, we first need it to have a UV layout.

UV Mapping

Let's go to the UV workspace (Figure 4-50) and have our game asset UV mapped. First, I choose the rook in layout workspace (but you can also do this in 3D viewport ➤ Object Mode) and then go to UV editing and choose Smart UV project under the UV header menu, and ta-da!

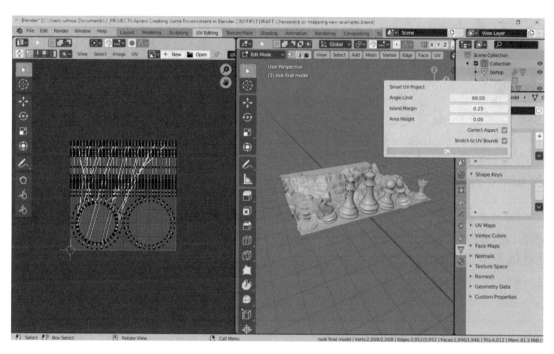

Figure 4-50. *UV Mapping process*

We already have a UV layout ready as shown in Figure 4-51.

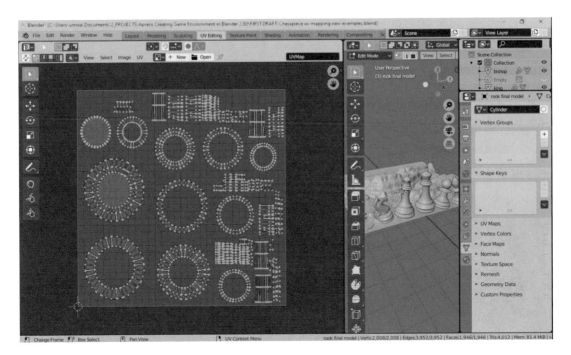

Figure 4-51. *UV Mapping process 2*

Even though we already have a UV layout presented after the Smart UV project, we need to take a look at some things like overlapping UVs. We can so this by going to Select menu ➤ Select Overlap.

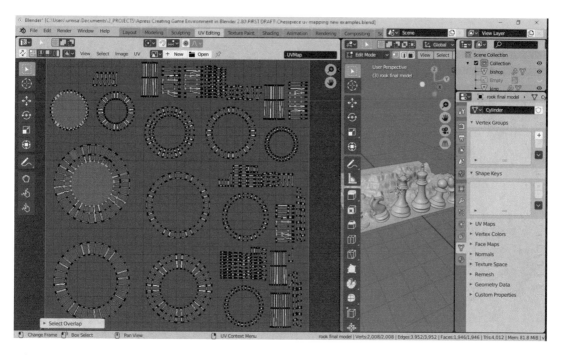

Figure 4-52. *UV Mapping process 3*

We can see in Figure 4-52 some of the overlapping UVs. What I do is to first take a closer look in order to know how should they be placed before I move those overlapping UVs.

Figure 4-53 shows the new UV layout with more spaces between UV islands and without overlapping UVs.

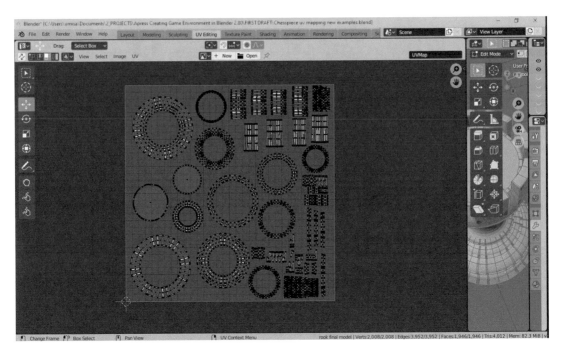

Figure 4-53. *UV Mapping process 4*

I also use Smart UV project for king, knight, pawn, queen, bishop, and for our landscape. Take a look at Figure 4-54 to see their UV layouts.

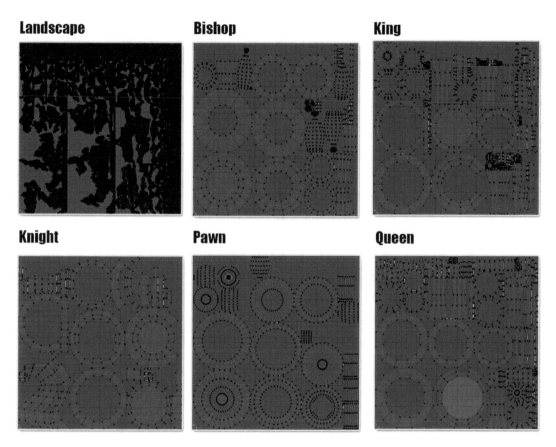

Landscape   **Bishop**   **King**

Knight   **Pawn**   **Queen**

Figure 4-54. *UV Mapping process 5*

You can see the different UV layouts created from the Smart UV project in this sample project that we have. For the landscape, remember that what we used in creating the landscape is an add-on and by default already has many vertices that result in having a lot of UVs presented in the UV layout. In this case, to make sure we don't have overlapping UVs, just use the select overlap; but we should avoid these kinds of crowded UVs as much as possible.

Now, we still have two more assets to UV mapped, and I used a different technique here. Take a look at Figure 4-55 to see our next process.

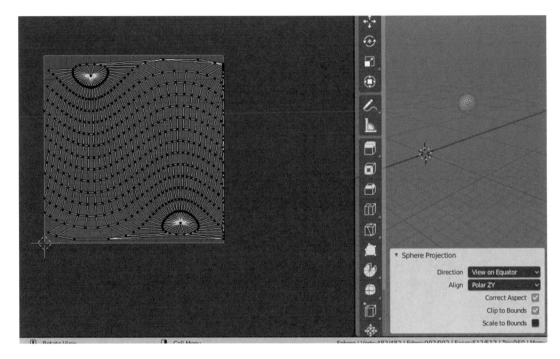

Figure 4-55. *UV Mapping process 6*

What you can see here is that I use the sphere projection for UV mapping of our two spheres. Since there are also some overlapping issues here, I move some of the UV faces.

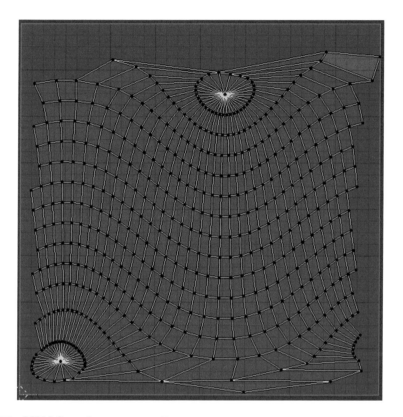

Figure 4-56. *UV Mapping process 7*

Figure 4-56 is the final output of UV layout for our spheres. I move the upper and lower parts where there are overlapping issues and scale it overall to make sure the whole island is in the UV layout.

Mostly, my techniques in UV processing are the basic ones since my sample project is also basic. There are a lot of techniques that can help you in creating a UV layout to create a clean layout including the following:

- **Minimal Stretching** - It means that a UV map is appropriate to the face size on the mesh so that when you add texture, it isn't stretched.

- **No Overlapping UV islands** - Overlapping UV islands will result in undesirable results in textures. For example, the texture you use will not be exactly show in the mesh if you have overlapping UVs.

- **Using UV Square Add-on to straighten any distorted islands** - It will allow you to align UV islands to grids, and it makes things so much easier to straighten out and fit together.

- **Enough space between islands for edge padding when using mipmaps in a game engine.**

- **As average-sized islands are possible, compare to each other to avoid big or too-small texel density differences.** - Texel density is the resolution of the texture on a mesh.

- **Filling the square UV space completely without wasted space.** - This is important for the resolution of a texture.

- **Convenient and readable in 2D if ever that people will use a 2D program at any stage for this an asset**.

- When seaming, the best place to put it is in areas that are not going to be seen easily, which means the bottom edges or the back sides.

- Supporting edges can really help clean up difficult seams, especially for hard surface objects. This helps stop stretching the UV at these edges.

- Poles can cause texture distortions so try to avoid adding seams on edges that end with poles.

- Things like clothes often have natural seams in them, and you would be in the right 80% of the time just using those natural seams.

Now, we're done with UV mapping, let's proceed with texturing.

Texturing

First things first, let's start texturing the landscape. I select the landscape asset and add our material base color (Figure 4-57). I select pure white as our material base color.

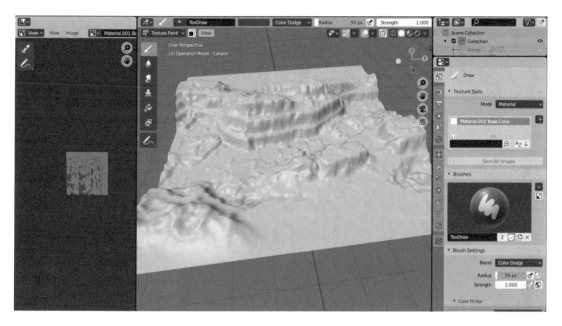

Figure 4-57. *Landscape Texturing Process*

I start added our first blending color (Figure 4-58). And I do this in the image editor since it will be easier to paint the overall landscape using the image editor, and with this, the overlapping UVs of the landscape can easily be covered or will not affect our texturing very much.

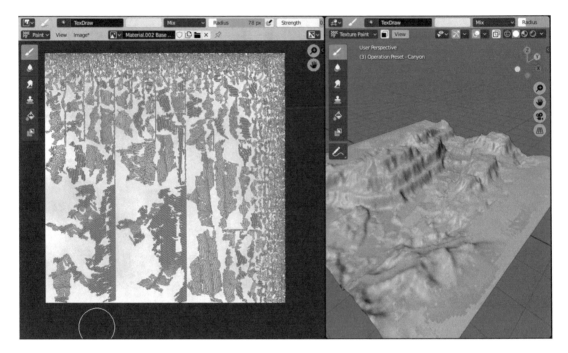

Figure 4-58. *Landscape Texturing Process*

Take a look at Figure 4-59 to see our output for the landscape asset.

Figure 4-59. *Landscape Texturing Process*

In the meantime, this is the output for our landscape. What I did here is I only used mix blending mode and just changed the radius and strength from time to time according to my own preferences. It depends on the other assets and processes, and this might be enhanced for the sake of our overall design.

Let's now proceed to texture our chess pieces.

I start the chess piece texturing with the pawn. For this one, I first used the fill tool and directly filled the gradient color in the image editor. You can make the gradient work by clicking at one corner, then dragging your mouse cursor to another corner. For the setting of filling in the properties, I use radial for gradient fill mode and choose the light blue and white colors. Figure 4-60 shows that even though I choose light blue and white colors in the properties setting, the output is kind of purple. This is because if you look at our settings for blend mode at the header settings, it was set to exclusion with the color near to purple. That's why our result color turns to a purple gradient.

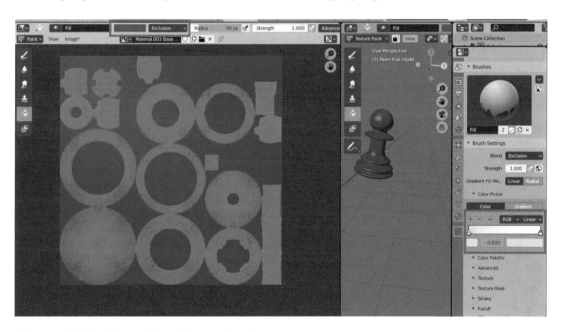

Figure 4-60. *Chess Piece Texturing Process*

I add another blending color using our draw tool in Image editor using soft light blend mode with a color in the range of green. The output color, as you can see in Figure 4-61, is blue with a combination of light blue. In soft light, when you paint over the part where you will paint the soft light blend mode, you will see another color just like in our sample project. As I paint around, the first color to see with soft light is the blue color, but as I paint over with it, the light blue color appears.

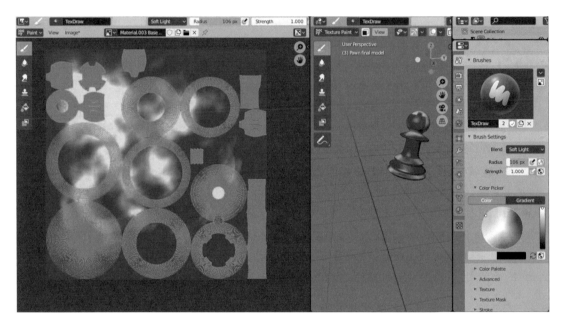

Figure 4-61. *Chess Piece Texturing Process*

I then use the smear tool to add an effect to our coloring (Figure 4-62). I also directly use the tool in 3D viewport to soften some of the edges that were created by the parts of the UV layout or the division of the mesh.

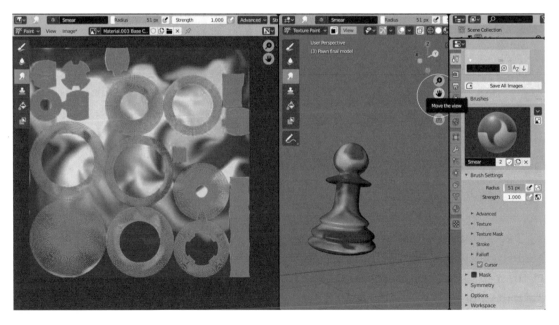

Figure 4-62. *Chess Piece Texturing Process*

I add a color in the range of pink using a draw tool with the screen blending mode directly in the image editor, and then I use the smear tool directly to the mesh in 3D viewport to blend the colors and add an effect; our output is shown in Figure 4-63.

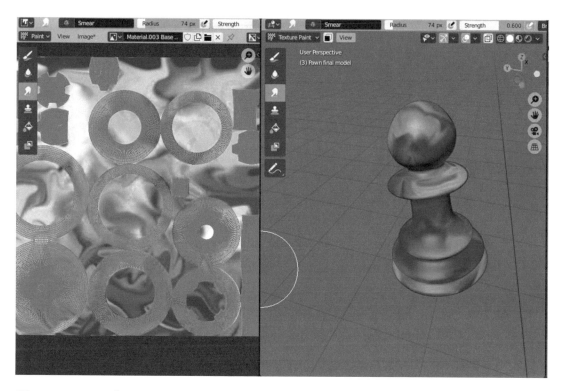

Figure 4-63. *Chess Piece Texturing Process*

Let's continue to our other pieces. For bishop, I used a fill tool also directly in the Image editor to create the first blend color. Then I used a different blending mode by adding other blend colors like Saturation, Value, Add, and Color Dodge. Then I directly blend the colors using the smear tool. Figure 4-64 shows the results.

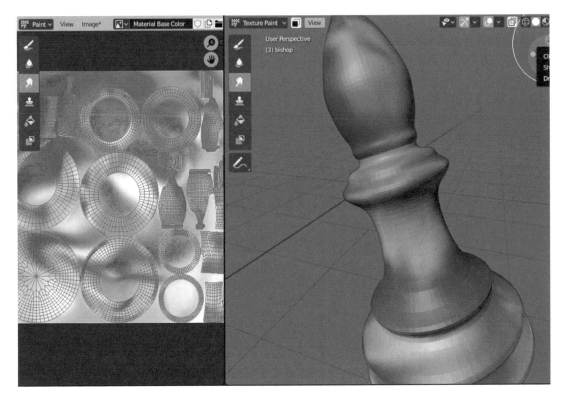

Figure 4-64. *Chess Piece Texturing Process*

Next, we have our rook. I use the same process with the rook. I use the fill tool to create a gradient color with red, pink, and purple; then I add white colors using the draw tool with a lighten blend mode. For the finale, I use a smear tool directly to the mesh to blend the colors and smoothen the edges that were created by the corners of the UVs.

But wait, we have two rooks here. It will be troublesome if we have to repaint this won't it? Well, there's a solution out there. Take a look at Figure 4-65 to see the process.

Figure 4-65. *Chess Piece Texturing Process*

First, you just select the mesh you will have your material with, and for this project that will be the other rook. Then go to the material panel in the properties editor, click the icon beside the new button, and choose the material you want to reuse and voilà! Your mesh is already textured (Figure 4-66). You just need to check if something is need to edit such as if there is a need to smooth in the blending of colors, etc.

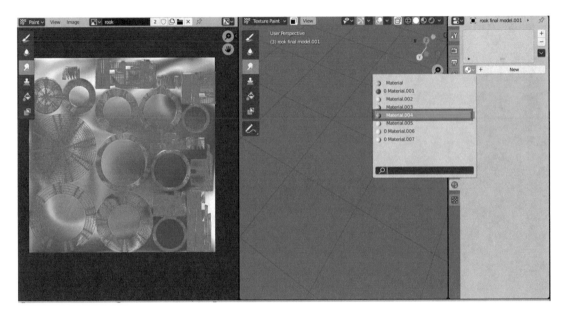

Figure 4-66. *Chess Piece Texturing Process*

Now, let's proceed with our texturing process and take a look at Figure 4-67 to see the output for the rest of our game assets.

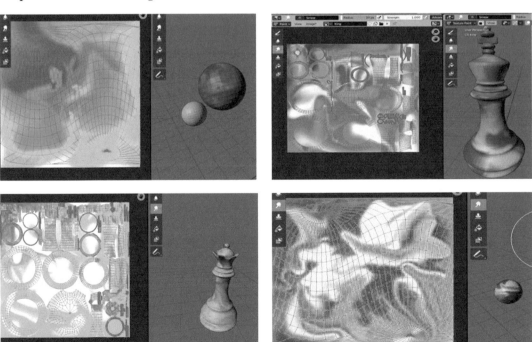

Figure 4-67. *Chess Piece Texturing Process*

For the knight, I used the same material as we used in the landscape. For the rest of the assets, we use the same method: Using the fill tool, choose a gradient for applying the first blend color and then use the draw tool together with another blend mode such as color dodge to create effects. Then use the smear tool for blending colors and smoothing sharp edges created by UV layouts in the textures.

Now, let's take a look at Figure 4-68 to see our final output for this texturing process.

Figure 4-68. *Final Output for Texturing process*

Now, let's proceed to our next chapter and continue learning!

CHAPTER 5

The Finale

We're now in the final chapter of our book. Are you still having fun? I hope you are.

In this chapter, we are going to talk about the process of importing and exporting game assets in Blender 3D. We will also talk about some open source game engines available there that will work with our game assets and how to import our assets into these game engines. We will also talk a bit about some commonly used 3D file formats.

So, without any delay, let's get started!

Importing Game Assets in Blender

Let's start Chapter 5 with the process involving how to import game assets in Blender. Of course, before we import a game asset, we need first to take a look at file formats that our program supports.

For Blender, we have 10 file formats that are supported: Collada (.dae), Alembic (.abc), Motion Capture (.bvh), Scalable Vector Graphics (.svg), Stanford (.ply), Stl (.stl), FBX (.fbx), glTF 2.0 (.glb/.gltf), Wavefront (.obj), and X3D Extensible 3D (.x3d/.wrl).

Let's have a little discussion about each of these file formats.

.DAE file format is a 3D interchange file format used for exchanging digital assets between multiple graphics programs. It is based on the Collada or Collaborative Design Activity XML Schema, which is now owned by Autodesk. Collada was originally developed by Sony and is now jointly supported by Sony and the Khronos Group.

.ABC file format is an interchangeable computer graphics, open source file format developed by Sony Pictures Imageworks and Industrial Light & Magic. It supports the common geometric representations used in the industry, including polygon meshes, subdivision surfaces, parametric curves, NURBS patches, and particles. Alembic also has support for transforming hierarchies and cameras.

© Ezra Thess Mendoza Guevarra 2020
E. T. Mendoza Guevarra, *Creating Game Environments in Blender 3D*,
https://doi.org/10.1007/978-1-4842-6174-3_5

.BVH file format is an ASCII file format developed by Biovision as a standard format to save biped character motion data that contains motion capture data for three-dimensional characters. It is used by 3D animation programs to import rotational joint data. BVH files also store animation data for characters in Second Life and other various 3D video games.

.SVG file format is a graphics file that uses a two-dimensional vector graphic format created by the World Wide Web Consortium (W3C). It describes images using a text format that is based on XML. SVG files are developed as a standard format for displaying vector graphics on the web.

.PLY file format is a three-dimensional image file created using the polygon file format, which is an open standard that describes objects as a collection of polygons. It contains a header followed by a list of vertices that specify the shape of each polygon. Since the PLY file format was developed at Stanford University, it is also known as the Stanford Triangle Format.

.FBX file format is a 2D or 3D drawing saved in the Autodesk FBX format. It maintains the full fidelity and functionality of the original file and can be manipulated by multiple programs. It is used for creating interoperability between 3D applications.

.GLTF 2.0 (Graphics Library Transmission Format) is a file format developed by the Khronos Group for 3D scenes and 3D models using the JSON standard. It stores a full scene description in JSON format, which includes node hierarchies, cameras, and materials. GLTF files also contain descriptor information about animation and meshes.

GLTF files can be used to save and share digital assets between different 3D modeling tools, like .DAE files. However, they are also optimized for download speed and load time at runtime, which makes it easier to use in mobile and web-based 3D modeling programs. It is also a more streamlined format for uploading and downloading from online digital asset databases.

.GLB is a binary form of gltf that includes textures instead of referencing them as external images.

.OBJ file format is a standard 3D image format that can be exported and opened by various 3D image editing programs. It contains a three-dimensional object that includes 3D coordinates, texture maps, polygonal faces, and other object information. This format is considered to be a universal 3D model format since it is widely supported by 3D image editing applications. The format is simple and text-based, which is one reason why many programs use it. Since the OBJ format is widely supported, many users export their models as OBJ files when transferring them from one 3D program to another or when sharing a 3D model with a coworker.

.X3D file format is an ISO-ratified file format and runtime architecture to represent and communicate 3D scenes and objects. This file format was developed by the Web3D Consortium and has evolved from its beginning as the Virtual Reality Modeling Language (VRML) to the considerably more mature, refined ISO X3D standard. It provides a system for the storage, retrieval, and playback of real-time 3D scenes in multiple applications.

.WRL file format is a virtual world created in VRML and can be navigated in three dimensions. WRL files are saved in an ASCII text format, which can be edited with a text editor.

Now, we have at least a basic idea about our file formats. So let's take a look at how to import our game assets using some of these file formats.

Importing Using .DAE Format

Let's take a look at Figures 5-1 to 5-6 to see the process of importing a .DAE file format.

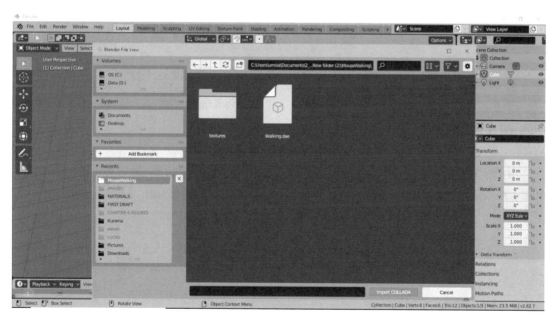

Figure 5-1. *Process of Importing .Dae part 1*

Of course, the first part will be to go to File menu ➤ Import ➤ choose COLLADA .dae ➤, then browsing to the folder where your .Dae file is located.

Usually, this file is downloaded in a compressed format like Zip. You can uncompress it using programs like Winrar or Winzip.

You can see in Figure 5-1 that we have a Walking.dae file, and beside it is a textures folder. Let's start importing our Walking.dae file.

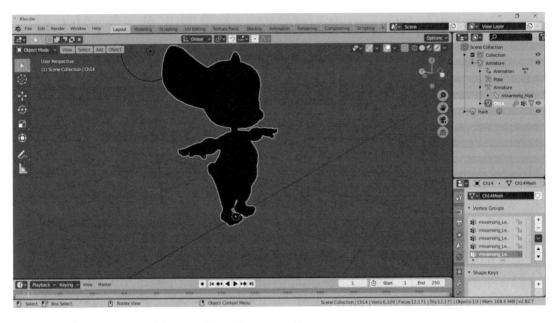

Figure 5-2. *Process of Importing .Dae part 2*

Ta-da! This is how your object looks like after you import it. Hmmm. We are already in the render view but we can't see any textures. Look, we even have a point light there. What's the problem? Okay. Let's take a look at our shaders editor.

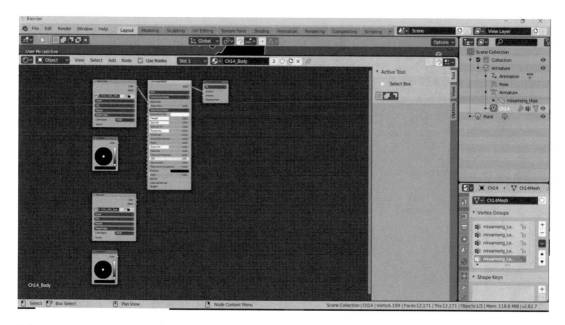

Figure 5-3. *Process of Importing .Dae part 3*

Hmmm. It seems that Blender isn't recognizing the nodes settings that the .DAE file format imported. This is why we have separate texture references for a .DAE file. In case the program didn't recognize your material shading, you can re-create it with your own shading settings.

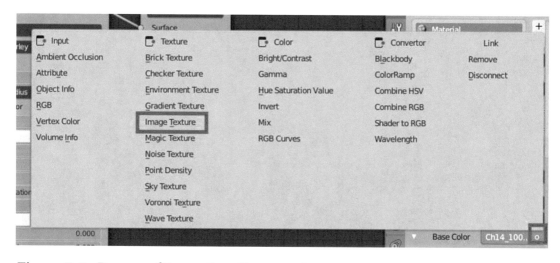

Figure 5-4. *Process of Importing .Dae part 4*

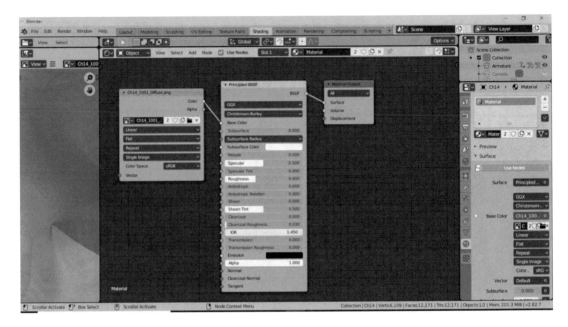

Figure 5-5. *Process of Importing .Dae part 5*

I replace the default node that our imported object is using by first creating another one, and then in the base color in properties from the material panel, I select the image texture and the texture provided with our .DAE file.

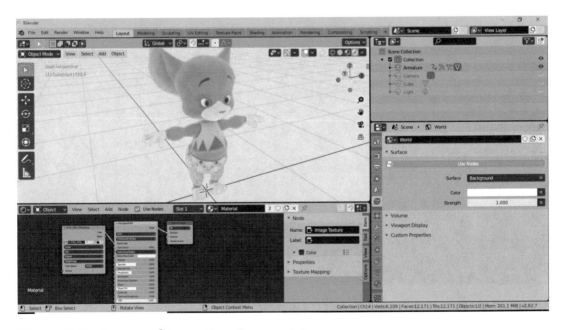

Figure 5-6. *Process of Importing .Dae part 6*

After fixing some things, as you can see in Figure 5-6, you are looking at our textures in a render view.

Let's proceed to our next file format.

Importing Using .ABC Format

Now, let's take a look at Figures 5-7 to 5-13 to see the process of importing an Alembic file.

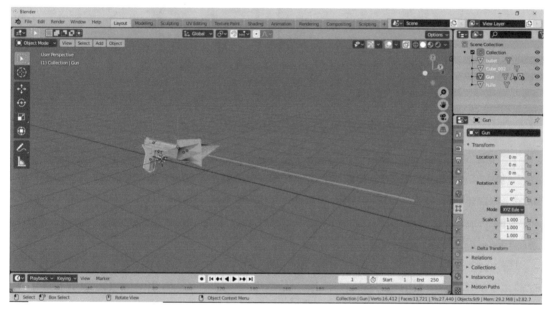

Figure 5-7. *Process of Importing .ABC file part 1*

Of course, the process will be the same as the first part. We will go to File menu ➤ Import ➤ Choose Alembic (.abc) ➤ Browse to the file location of our file to be imported, and then import.

What we can see in Figure 5-7 is the view of our game asset after being imported. Our texture for this one is separated so if we look at the render view, we can only see a diffuse color white as a material shade of the gun. Let's add the texture of the gun.

Okay. If you are a beginner, you might wonder about the form of our gun. Why is that there that long line or cylinder, and how can we ever hide it? You can just play around in the outliner and hide parts of your game asset to know which one is the one on your screen.

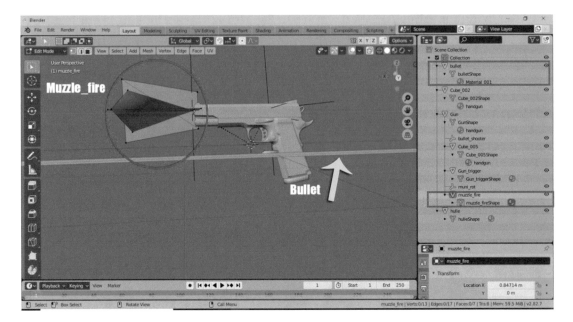

Figure 5-8. *Process of Importing .ABC file part 2*

You can see that the named muzzle_fire object in our outliner refers to that mesh encircled in our gun, and the bullet refers to the long line. If you don't want to see these parts in your render or you feel that you don't need those parts of your imported game asset, all you need to do is to go to your outliner and hide those unwanted parts of your game assets by filtering it out.

If you just want to disable it in the viewport, all you just need to do is to click the eye icon next to the object name; but if you want to remove it in the render view but you don't want to delete that part completely, you need to go to Filter ➤ toggle renders, which will enable you to manipulate which object will be in the render.

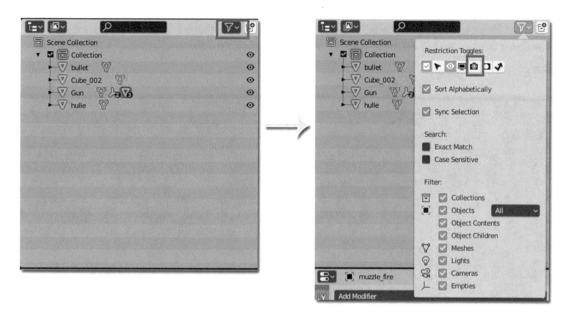

Figure 5-9. *Filtering*

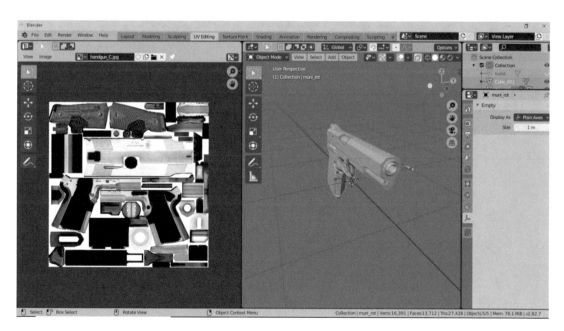

Figure 5-10. *Process of Importing .ABC file part 3*

In order to apply the textures, first I select all the mesh that can be seen in the viewport and go to UV editing. I go to UV editor and open the texture that I will use for the gun.

Figure 5-11. *Process of Importing .ABC file part 4*

The next thing I do is to go to texture paint to add the texture by selecting the mode to single image and selecting the texture I want for the gun as the single image material.

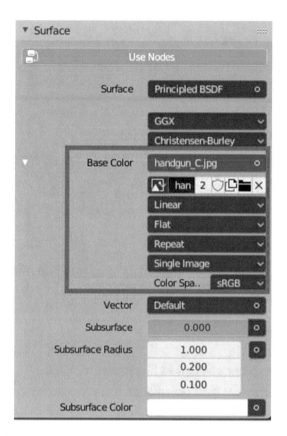

Figure 5-12. *Material settings*

Make sure that your base color in your material settings has the image or texture name in it. Sometimes, even you already have the texture in the texture paint or even a UV wrapping, the image doesn't link to this part; that's why the texture didn't appear in the render view.

Figure 5-13. *Render View*

This is now how our game asset looks like in render view.

Let's now proceed with our next file format.

Importing Using .OBJ Format

.OBJ file format comes with an .Mtl file format; it's the file format that contains data about the materials of the object.

Let's now take a look at Figures 5-14 to 5-17 to see the process of importing an .OBJ file.

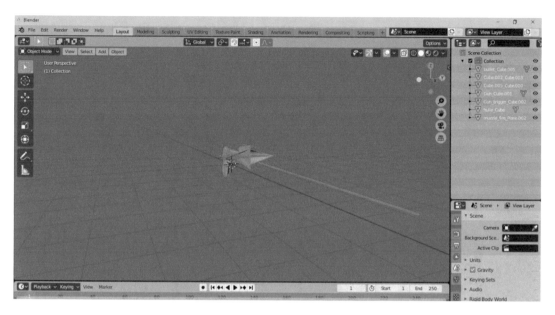

Figure 5-14. *Process of importing .Obj file part 1*

The first part of the process is of course the same: File Menu ➤ Import ➤ Wavefront (.obj) ➤ browse your file ➤ then import.

Again, we will filter out what part of our game asset we want to be seen and rendered.

You might wonder how to import the .Mtl file that comes with the .Obj file. When you import the .Obj file, Blender will also import the associated .Mtl file by default as well as long as they have the same file name.

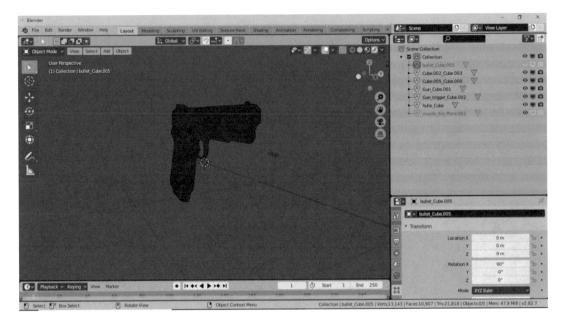

Figure 5-15. *Process of importing .Obj file part 2*

We already know that the .Mtl files are already applied. Then why we can't see any textures in our mesh, but instead, we see it in pink? It's because just like what we did in the Alembic file, we need to select the meshes and unwrap them to the UV editor with the texture that we want to use in it.

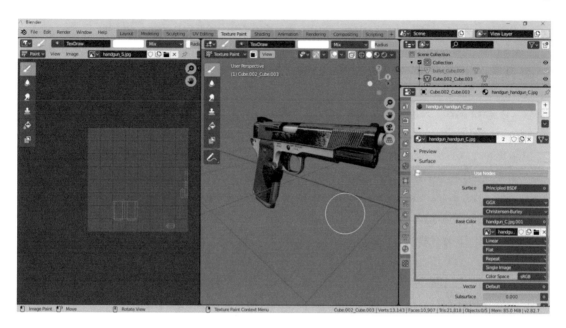

Figure 5-16. *Process of importing .Obj file part 3*

We also need to re-browse the file in the material settings since the textures or the reference images now have a new path.

Figure 5-17. *Render View*

Here is the rendered view of our game asset imported from the .Obj file.

The process of importing an FBX file is the same with .DAE and .ABC. You just need to go to File menu ➤ import ➤ browse the .FBX file and import. That's it. If there is a need to do something with textures, just look at the material settings like what we did in the .DAE and .ABC files, but if you have an .FBX file with textures in it, it will be easier. You just need to import it and everything is already done.

It's the same thing with a .PLY file. You just need to go File Menu ➤ Import ➤ Stanford (.Ply) ➤ Browse .Ply file ➤ import your file and then that's it. It's the same for both .STL and .WRL files but with the same set of concerns. If your mesh is something like our gun with some added meshes that aren't necessary, you might need to edit something before you can use it.

Even for .glTF files, you just need to go to File Menu ➤ Import ➤ glTF 2.0 (.gltf/.glb) ➤ browse a glTF file ➤ import your file and that's it. When you render, you can even see your materials in it even the textures are created in a separated folder.

For .SVG files, it is the same process. The only difference will be is that when you import .SVG files, they will end up as curve objects since they were originally 2D images.

For .BVH files, it is also the same simple process of importing as .FBX, after all. What we have in this file format is only the animation data of your project as you can see in Figures 5-18 and 5-19.

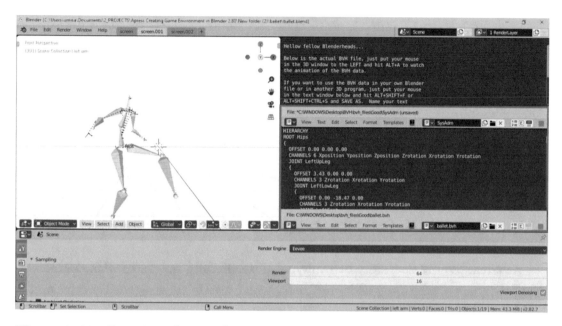

Figure 5-18. *Creation of .BVH data in Blender. Credit to centralsource.com*

The one I boxed with the red rectangle is the .BVH data created inside the .Blend file or in Blender. The one you can see in the 3D viewport is the output using this data.

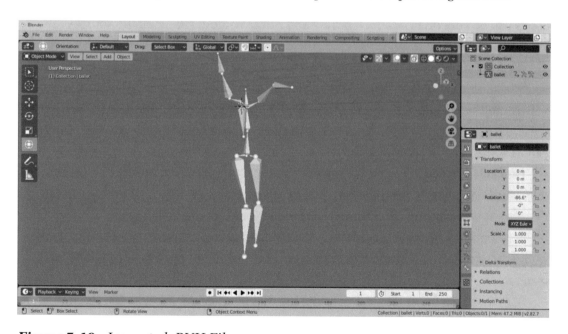

Figure 5-19. *Imported .BVH File*

In Figure 5-19, this is how it looks like after you import a .BVH file. This is the same as the one in Figure 5-18.

Now, we're done discussing the process of importing our game assets in Blender. Let's now talk about exporting our game assets from Blender.

Exporting Game Assets in Blender

For exporting game assets, we also have 10 available file formats, which are COLLADA (.dae), Alembic (.abc), Universal Scene Description (.usd, .usdc, .usda), Motion Capture (.bvh), Stanford (.ply), Stl (.stl), FBX (.fbx), glTF 2.0 (.glb/.gltf), Wavefront (.obj), and X3D Extensible 3D (.x3d)

We already know .dae, .abc, .bvh, .ply, .stl, .fbx, .glb/.gltf, .obj, and .x3d file formats. What's left here are the .usd, .usdc, and .usda, which are Universal Scene Descriptions. Let's have a little discussion about this file format.

.USD is a file format that can be both ASCII and binary-encoded. It was developed by Pixar in a Universal Scene Description, which is a framework for interchange in 3D computer graphics data. This characteristic of .USD files are advantageous in certain scenarios like if one has a USD file that contains references to plain .usd assets, those assets can be converted between binary and ASCII without changing the sources that refer to them.

Now, let's talk about the process of exporting files. The process of exporting in all file formats in Blender are the same. You just need to go to File Menu ➤ Export ➤ file format you wanted ➤ to export the game assets. The only difference lies after you export the file and for some file formats, there are some settings available in case you want only to export some parts of your project.

For Collada (.Dae) files, you only have the simple exportation process. There are no other settings available. Its difference is that the textures are separated to the .dae file that contains the information about the geometry, etc., of the object.

For Alembic (.abc) files, it also only has the simple exportation process and no other settings available; in addition, it only has the .abc file and no other separated file for its textures.

For Wavefront (.obj) files, we have the file that handles the information for our object, which is the .obj file and a file that handles the information for our materials, which is the .mtl file. It also has other export settings available.

For .Universal Scene Description (.usd, .usda, .usdc) files, it has other export settings but it doesn't have a separated file for its textures. This is the same for .PLY, .FBX, .GLB, .STL, and .X3D. Now, let's take a look at Figure 5-20 to see the other settings that we have for exporting our game assets in a .usd file.

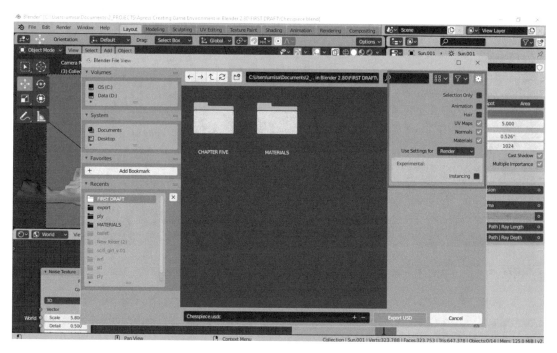

Figure 5-20. *Exporting with .usd file format*

You can see in Figure 5-20 that we have options to include the animation, hair, UV maps, normals, and materials. We also have an option to just export those currently selected objects in the scene or project, and we can do this by toggling the **selection only**. You can also choose which settings it will be based on, in the settings of your project in the render mode or in the viewport mode. By default, exporting UV maps, normals, and materials are enabled.

Now, let's look at Figure 5-21 to see the other settings that we have for exporting our game assets in a .PLY file format.

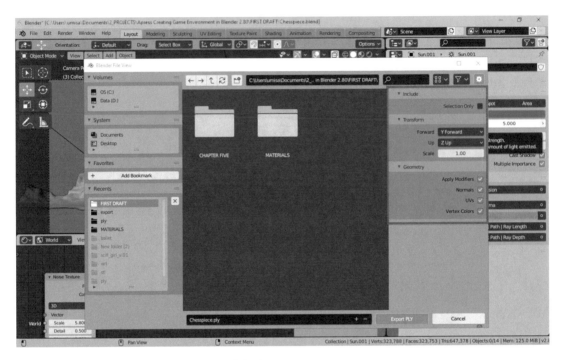

Figure 5-21. *Exporting with .ply file format*

As you can see in Figure 5-21, we have options for including modifiers' settings, normals, UVs, and vertex colors in exportation. We also have an option if we want only those that are currently selected in the project to be the ones that will be exported; and we can do this by toggling the **selection only** under the include panel. In **transform**, this part will help you set your game assets' positions differently from what it is in the project. The forward and up refers to the axis while the scale refers to the size of the game assets after you export them.

Let's now have the .STL file format. Take a look at Figure 5-22 to see the other options for this file format when exporting our game assets.

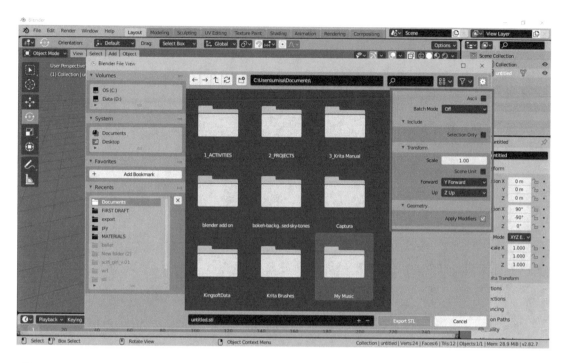

Figure 5-22. *Exporting with .stl file format*

For .STL format, we have an option to include modifiers' settings. We also have the option to transform our game assets' positioning after the exportation just like what we have in .PLY file format; and an option if we want to export only the current selected objects in our project by toggling the **selection only**.

Let's see what additional options for exporting game assets that we have for the .FBX file format in Figure 5-23.

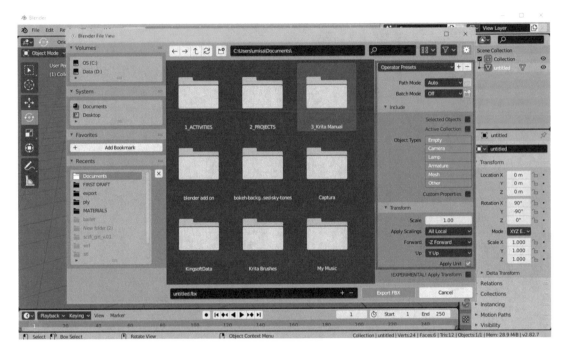

Figure 5-23. *Exporting with .fbx file format*

For .fbx file format, we have more specific options for exporting our game assets. For object types, we can choose if we want to export empties, cameras, lamps or light objects, armatures or the bones that we use for animation or rigging, mesh, and other object types like curves. We still have the option if we want only to export those that are currently selected in the project, and we can do this by toggling the **selected objects**. We also have another option if we only want to export those that are part of the active collection and we can do this by toggling **active collection**. We have here the transform panel, which gives us option if we want to change the position in the axis or scale the game assets after exportation. There are other options there that are for geometry of the mesh (under the geometry panel), armature and animation.

Under the geometry panel, you can decide about the smoothing information: if it will be only normals, faces, or edges. You also have the option here to export the subdivision surface, loose edges, and tangent space.

Under the armature panel, you can set the axis for the primary and the secondary bones. There is also this option called Only Deform Bones, which enable you to export only the deformed Bones and the Non-deformed bones that have a deformed children(bones).

Now, let's take a look at the settings of exportation that we have for .GLB file format in Figure 5-24.

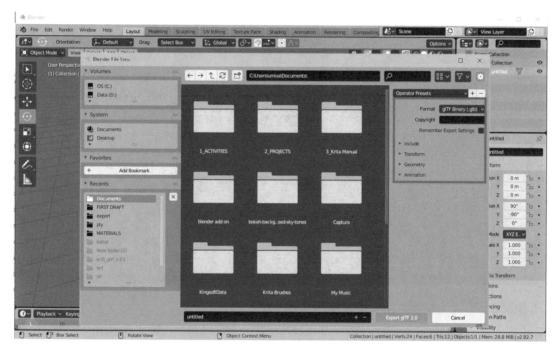

Figure 5-24. *Exporting with .glb file format*

Hmmm. As for .glb format, you can see in Figure 5-24 that we have **remember export settings**. As what it says, if you toggle this up, whatever settings you have, they will be saved and that will be the one Blender uses as export settings the next time you export a game asset unless you change it again. And another thing, we have here **copyright** where you can place a copyright setting.

There are still options for which objects you wanted to be exported, and that was under the include panel. Also, the option for the positioning of your game assets after exportation was under the transform panel. You also have options if you want to include modifiers' settings, UVs, normals, tangents, vertex colors, and materials, and these are all under the geometry panel. What you can see under the animation panel are options if you want to export information related to shape keys, skinning, and, of course, animation.

Now, let's take a look at Figure 5-25 to see the available export settings for the .X3D file format.

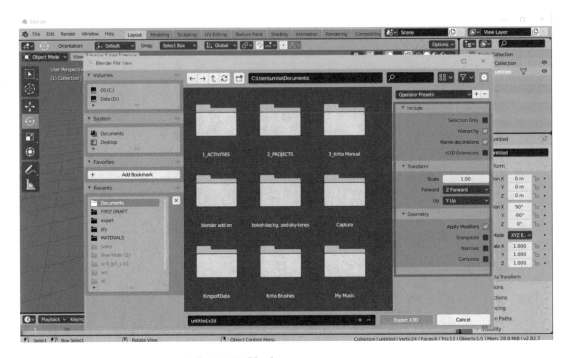

Figure 5-25. *Exporting with .X3D file format*

As for .X3D file format, still, we have an option to include modifiers' settings, triangulate, normals, and compress. We also have the option to change the position and size of our game assets after exportation through the settings under the transform panel. We still have this **selection only**, which gives us the option to only export those objects that are currently selected in the project. We also have this **hierarchy** that when enabled exports parent–child relationships of the objects while **name decoration** adds prefixes to the names of exported nodes to indicate their type.

Let's take a look at the export settings of the .OBJ file format shown in Figure 5-26.

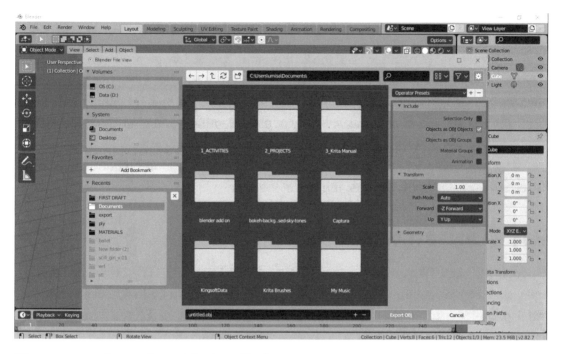

Figure 5-26. *Exporting with .OBJ file format*

For .OBJ file format, we have **selection only**, which gives us the options to export only the currently selected objects in the project; **objects as OBJ objects**, which gives us the option to exports objects in objects under OBJ file format; **objects as OBJ groups** that give us the option to export objects in groups under OBJ file format; **material groups** that give us the option to export our game assets' materials in the group; and **animation**, which gives us the option to write out an .OBJ for each frame.

We also have options here for adjusting the size and position of our game assets in the axis after exporting under the transform panel. And we also have options here if we want to include modifiers' settings, normals, UVs, materials, triangulate faces, curves, etc., and this is under the geometry panel.

Now that we're already discussed how our game assets can be exported in different file formats, let's start discussing how we can import our game assets in a game engine that is compatible with Blender.

Open Source Game Engine

The earlier version of Blender, until the 2.7x version, has its own game engine; but when 2.80 came, Mr. Ton Roosendaal decided to discontinue it. He stated that the future of the Blender game engine will integrate the system into Blender as an interaction mode for game prototypes, architectural walkthroughs, and scientific simulation. Now, Blender is working to be a good support for external open source game engines.

Now, let's start our brief discussion about one of the open source game engines that we can use together with Blender, the Godot Engine.

Godot Engine (godotengine.org)

Godot is a 2D and 3D game engine released under an MIT license. It's both a free and open source game engine. Its development was started by Juan 'reduz' Linietsky and Ariel 'punto' Manzur in 2007. Godot aims to offer a fully integrated game development environment. It allows developers to create a game from scratch, needing no tools beyond those used for content creation like art assets, music, etc.

Godot engine is a feature-packed, cross-platform game engine to create 2D and 3D games from a unified interface. It provides a comprehensive set of common tools, so users can focus on making games without having to reinvent the wheel. Games can be exported in one click to a number of platforms, including the major desktop platforms (Linux, masOS, and Windows) as well as mobile (Android, iOS) and web-based (HTML5) platforms.

Godot is a free and open source software under the OSI-approved MIT licensed. In short, you are free to download and use it for any purpose, personal, nonprofit, commercial, or otherwise. You are also free to modify, distribute, redistribute, and remix Godot for any reason, both noncommercially and commercially.

The official supported languages for Godot are GDScript, Visual Scripting, C#, and C++. If you are just starting out with either Godot or game development in general, GDscript is the recommended language to learn and use since it is native to Godot. While scripting languages tend to be less performant than lower-level languages in the long run, for prototyping, developing Minimum Viable Products (MVPs) and focusing on Time-To-Market (TTM), GDScript will provide a fast, friendly, and capable way of developing your games.

Godot also includes a script editor with a real-time parser, syntax highlighting, and code completion. It also features a built-in debugger that helps you explore and modify your project while it's running, a built-in profiler with graph plotting and time seeking, and an error logger with full stack traces.

Godot also has support for physical-based rendering with full MSAA support, full-principled BSDF with subsurface scattering, reflection, refraction, anisotropy, clear coat, transmittance, etc. It also uses global illumination for real-time gorgeous graphics, easy-to-use shader language based on GLSL with a built-in editor and code completion, and mid- and post-processing effects including a new tonemapper that supports HDR, multiple standard curves and auto-exposure, screen space reflections, fog, bloom, and depth of field.

Okay. We already have basic knowledge about Godot's features and capabilities. Let's now see its process for importing our game assets. Take a look at Figure 5-27 to 5-32 to see the process of importing game assets to the Godot game engine.

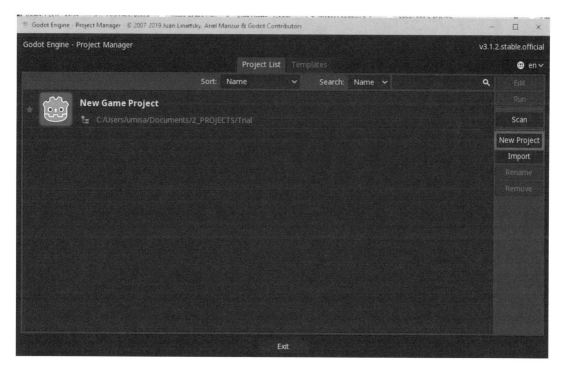

Figure 5-27. *Godot importing process 1*

I export our game assets in Blender in a .gITF file format. The only file formats you can import in Godot engine are .OBJ, glTF 2.0, .DAE, ESCN, and .FBX, but there are problems with .FBX since it is a proprietary file format and .OBJ is pretty limited because there is no support for pivots, skeletons, etc. And for .DAE, the supported ones are more of the older versions. The most recommended file format would be the glTF 2.0. So, for our project, I will also use the glTF 2.0 format.

Now, we're going to import it in Godot, but first, we need to create a project in the said game engine. What you can see in Figure 5-27 is the first window you can see when you open Godot. When creating a new project, you just need to click New project, but if you already have an existing Godot project, either you will choose it in the list or you will choose the Import button if the project is not in the list that appears in the window.

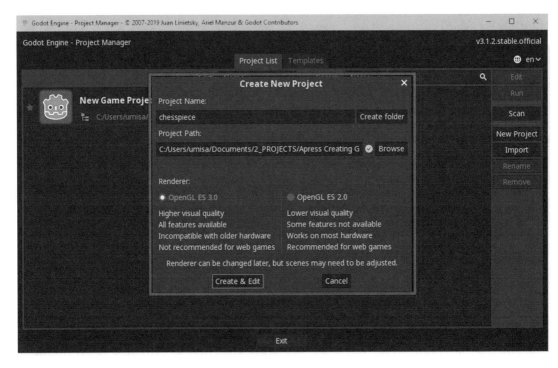

Figure 5-28. *Godot importing process 2*

Next, we will be asked for the project name. Godot isn't sensitive for a project name, but for project path, it requires an empty folder so you will need to create a new folder that is specific to a Godot project.

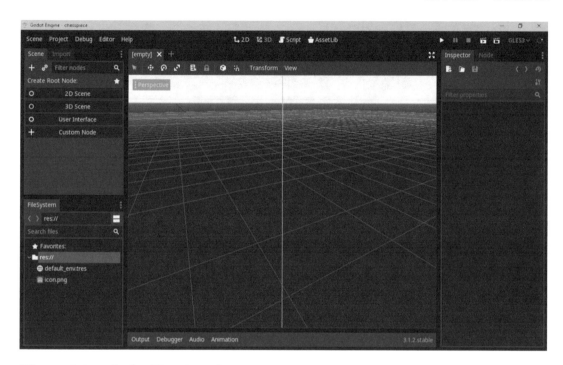

Figure 5-29. *Godot User Interface*

You can see in Figure 5-29 the interface of the Godot game engine. It looks simple, right? But it is actually kind of tricky. When you created a new folder for your project earlier, Godot created files with it just like what you can see in Figure 5-30.

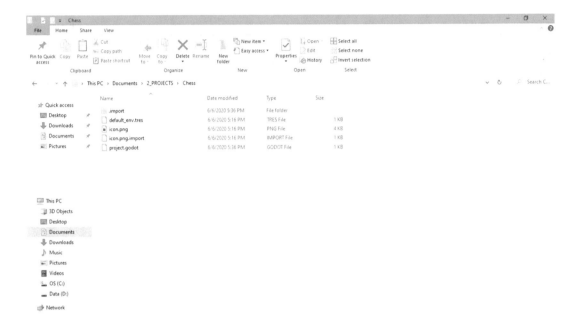

Figure 5-30. *Project folder for Godot*

You can notice that the default_env.tres and icon.png can also be seen in Godot's file system panel. Now, for us to be able to import our object, all we need to do is to copy and paste our object or our glTF 2.0 file in this folder.

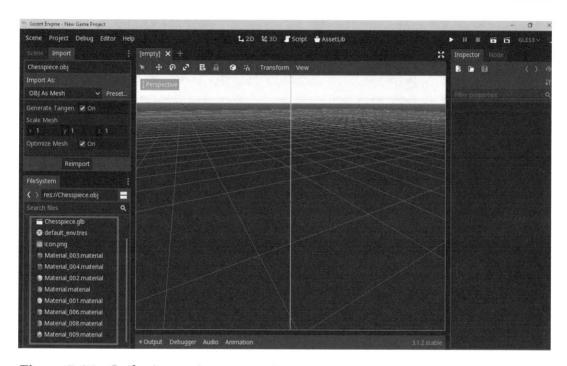

Figure 5-31. *Godot importing process 3*

This will be the next thing that happens after you import your game assets. You will see in the FileSystem panel the .glb file, together with the material files of your object. If you look at your folder, you can also see a file equivalent to those that you can see in this FileSystem panel. In other words, whatever you do in this panel will affect your project folder, and whatever you do in your project folder will also have an effect on this panel.

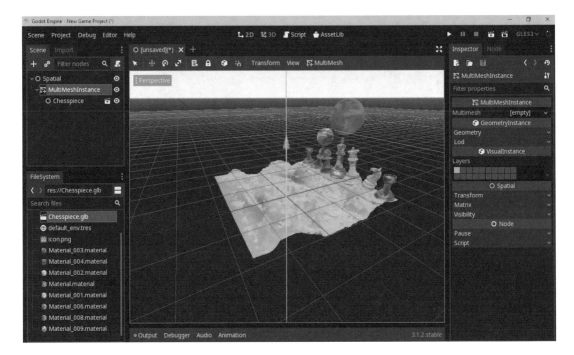

Figure 5-32. *Godot importing process 4*

In order to use our imported game assets, we need to use so-called instances. To do this, you first need to create a root node in the scene panel. Godot gives four options there: 2D scene, 3D scene, user interface, and custom node. Since we're doing 3D, we will choose 3D scene. After clicking 3D scene, you will see "Spatial" created. Next, you will click the plus icon to choose instances or nodes for our object to work on. Since we want to create a mesh one, we will click MultiMeshInstance. After adding the instance, you can just drag your game asset to the viewport and voilà! Your game asset will already appear in the scene.

These are the processes on how we import our game assets from Blender to a Godot game engine.

There are other open source game engines out there that can be used together with Blender. Here are some of those to help you find other options.

Stride (stride3d.net)

Stride, which is formerly known as Xenko, is a free and open source, highly modular, and super versatile game engine. It was originally developed by Silicon Studio and can be used to create mobile, PC and VR games, or as a high-end rendering engine for non-gaming applications such as architecture, medical, and engineering visualization software, training simulation, and so on.

Stride comes with a robust toolchain that enables you to intuitively and efficiently create, manage, and modify all assets of your game. The suite editors simplify and automate common development workflows. Its nested prefab and archetype systems scale along all editors and assets.

Stride's PBR materials, light probes, post effects, multi-threading, and next-gen graphics API support deliver realistic graphics with outstanding performance. The flexible pipeline, accessible low-level APIs, and customizable shaders let you tweak the rendering as much as you need.

It comes with a full set of modules dedicated to editing every part of your game. Each is provided out of the box and integrated into the engine. Modern C# scripting with shader and script hot reload lets you build prototypes and iterate fast.

Stride uses a single API for every device, with native support for Oculus and HTV Vive, and also, Stride's HRTF binaural audio greatly improves VR immersion.

Armory3D (armory3D.org)

Armory3D is an open source software with full Blender integration, which turns it into a complete game development tool. It offers a unified workflow from start to finish, making your work faster. There is no more jumping between different applications to constantly export data.

Behind the scenes, Armory3D is powered by open source technology. Utilizing Kha, a multimedia framework, and Haxe, a cross-platform toolkit, it provides first-class performance and portability.

Armory3D is based on the cycles nodes. Materials are precompiled into shaders suitable for real-time rendering. Every scene in Armory3D is renderable as-is in cycles using path tracing. This makes it possible to use cycles for light baking with no separate setup. Everything is bundled to provide ultimate game prototype templates. The code editor has integrated debugging support. You can use nodes, write scripts in Haxe, or embed WebAssembly code. You can also create live scenes and export them to desktop, web, and mobile consoles so everyone can experience them. A binary data format and asset robust animation system are employed, with support for GPU skinning, action blending, and events. On top of that, each node can be animated in a timeline using keyframes, just like you are used to.

Now, this concludes Chapter 5 as well as this book. I do hope that you learned something with this book. So, let's keep on learning!

APPENDIX A

HotKeys

General	
New	Ctrl N
Open	Ctrl O
Open Recent	Shift Ctrl O
Save	Ctrl S
Save As	Shift Ctrl S
Quit	Ctrl Q
Undo	Ctrl Z
Redo	Shift Ctrl Z
Add mesh/Add nodes	Shift A
Operator Search	F3
Render Image	F12
View Render	F11
Play Animation	Spacebar
Render Animation	Ctrl F12
View Animation	Ctrl F11
Opening Toolbar	T
Opening Sidebar	N

(continued)

© Ezra Thess Mendoza Guevarra 2020
E. T. Mendoza Guevarra, *Creating Game Environments in Blender 3D*,
https://doi.org/10.1007/978-1-4842-6174-3

General

Quick Favorites	Q
Mode Type Pie Menu	Ctrl Tab
Shading Type Pie Menu	Z
Move Objects to Collection	M
Create New Collection	Ctrl G
Select All	A
Undo Selection	Alt A
Invert Selection	Ctrl I
Circle Selection	C
Join Objects	Ctrl J
Insert Animation Keyframes	I
Delete Animation Keyframes	Alt I
Delete Objects	X
Hide Selected Objects	H
Show Hidden Objects	Alt H

Views/Navigation

Perspective/Orthographic	Numpad 5
Camera	Numpad 0
Top	Numpad 7
Bottom	Ctrl Numpad 7
Front	Numpad 1
Back	Ctrl Numpad 1

(continued)

General

Right	Numpad 3
Left	Ctrl Numpad 3
Orbit Left	Numpad 4
Orbit Right	Numpad 6
Orbit Up	Numpad 8
Orbit Down	Numpad 2
Orbit Opposite	Numpad 9
Pan Left	Ctrl Numpad 4
Pan Right	Ctrl Numpad 6
Pan Up	Ctrl Numpad 8
Pan Down	Ctrl Numpad 2
Roll Left	Shift Numpad 4
Roll Right	Shift Numpad 6
Zoom In	Numpad +
Zoom Out	Numpad -
Zoom Region	Shift B
Render Region	Ctrl B
Clear render Region	Ctrl Alt B
Toggle Quad View	Ctrl Alt Q
Toggle Maximize Area	Ctrl Spacebar
Toggle Fullscreen Area	Ctrl Alt Spacebar

(continued)

General

Switching Editors

File Browser	Shift F1
Movie Clip	Shift F2
Shade Editor	Shift F3
Python Console	Shift F4
3D View	Shift F5
Graph Editor	Shift F6
Properties	Shift F7
Video Sequencer	Shift F8
Outliner	Shift F9
Image Editor	Shift F10
Text Editor	Shift F11
Dope Sheet	Shift F12

Tools per Workspace/Editor/Modes

(To access Annotate tools by its own hotkeys, use Shift Spacebar D at first access)

Layout Workspace

Select	Shift + Spacebar + W
Select Box	Shift + Spacebar + B
Select Circle	Shift + Spacebar + C
Select Lasso	Shift + Spacebar + L
Cursor	Shift + Spacebar + Spacebar
Move	Shift + Spacebar + G

(continued)

General

Rotate	Shift + Spacebar + R
Scale	Shift + Spacebar + S
Scale Cage	Shift + Spacebar + 3
Transform	Shift + Spacebar + T
Annotate	Shift + Spacebar + D or 5
Annotate Line	Shift + Spacebar + D or 6
Annotate Polygon	Shift + Spacebar + D or 7
Annotate Eraser	Shift + Spacebar + D or 8
Measure	Shift + Spacebar + M

Modeling Workspace and Edit Mode

Extrude Region	Shift + Spacebar + E
Extrude Along Normals	Shift + Spacebar + 9
Extrude Individuals	Shift + Spacebar + 0
Extrude to Cursor	Shift + Spacebar + Shift 1
Inset Faces	Shift + Spacebar + I
Bevel	Shift + Spacebar + Ctrl + B
Loop Cut	Shift + Spacebar + Ctrl + R
Offset Edge Loop Cut	Shift + Spacebar + Shift + Ctrl + R
Knife	Shift + Spacebar + K
Bisect	Shift + Spacebar + Shift + 2
Polybuild	Shift + Spacebar + Shift + 3
Spin	Shift + Spacebar + Shift + 4
Spin Duplicate	Shift + Spacebar + Shift + 5

(continued)

General

Smooth	Shift + Spacebar + Shift + 6
Randomize	Shift + Spacebar + Shift + 7
Edge Slide	Shift + Spacebar + Shift + 8
Vertex Slide	Shift + Spacebar + Shift + V
Shrink/Flatten	Shift + Spacebar + Alt + S
Push/Pull	Shift + Spacebar + Shift + 9
Shear	Shift + Spacebar + Shift + Ctrl + Alt + S
To Sphere	Shift + Spacebar + Shift + Alt + S
Rip Region	Shift + Spacebar + V
Rip Edge	Shift + Spacebar + Alt + D
Annotate	Shift + Spacebar + D

Sculpting Workspace and Sculpt mode

Draw	Shift + Spacebar + X
Clay	Shift + Spacebar + C
Clay Stripes	Shift + Spacebar + 1
Layer	Shift + Spacebar + L
Inflate	Shift + Spacebar + I
Blob	Shift + Spacebar + 2
Crease	Shift + Spacebar + Shift + C
Smooth	Shift + Spacebar + S
Flatten	Shift + Spacebar + Shift + T
Fill	Shift + Spacebar + 3
Scrape	Shift + Spacebar + 4

(*continued*)

General

Pinch	Shift + Spacebar + P
Grab	Shift + Spacebar + G
Snake Hook	Shift + Spacebar + K
Thumb	Shift + Spacebar + 5
Nudge	Shift + Spacebar + 6
Rotate	Shift + Spacebar + 7
Simplify	Shift + Spacebar + 8
Mask	Shift + Spacebar + 9
Box Mask	Shift + Spacebar + B
Lasso Mask	Shift + Spacebar + 0
Box Hide	Shift + Spacebar + Shift + H
Annotate	Shift + Spacebar + Shift + 1
Annotate Line	Shift + Spacebar + Shift + 2
Annotate Polygon	Shift + Spacebar + Shift + 3
Annotate Eraser	Shift + Spacebar + Shift + 4

UV Editing Workspace (UV Editor)
(Select to Transform tool is the same as in Layout Workspace)

Select Box	Shift + Spacebar + B
Cursor	Shift + Spacebar + Spacebar
Move	Shift + Spacebar + G
Rotate	Shift + Spacebar + R
Scale	Shift + Spacebar + S
Transform	Shift + Spacebar + T

(continued)

General

Annotate Eraser	Shift + Spacebar + 6
Grab	Shift + Spacebar + 7
Relax	Shift + Spacebar + 8
Pinch	Shift + Spacebar + 9
Transform Tool	Shift + Spacebar + T

Texture Paint Workspace (Image Editor in Paint Mode)

Draw *(Same in Texture Paint mode)*	Shift + Spacebar + 1
Soften *(Same in Texture Paint mode)*	Shift + Spacebar + 2
Smear *(Same in Texture Paint mode)*	Shift + Spacebar + 3
Clone *(Same in Texture Paint mode)*	Shift + Spacebar + 4
Fill *(Same in Texture Paint mode)*	Shift + Spacebar + 5
Mask *(Same in Texture Paint mode)*	Shift + Spacebar + 6
Annotate *(Only in Texture Paint Mode)*	Shift + Spacebar + 7
Annotate Line *(Only in Texture Paint Mode)*	Shift + Spacebar + 8
Annotate Polygon *(Only in Texture Paint Mode)*	Shift + Spacebar + 9
Annotate Eraser *(Only in Texture Paint Mode)*	Shift + Spacebar + 0

(continued)

General

*Layout Workspace in Weight
Paint and Vertex Paint*

Draw (Weight Paint and Vertex Paint)	Shift + Spacebar + 1
Blur (Weight Paint and Vertex Paint)	Shift + Spacebar + 2
Average (Weight Paint and Vertex Paint)	Shift + Spacebar + 3
Smear (Weight Paint and Vertex Paint)	Shift + Spacebar + 4
Gradient (Weight Paint Only)	Shift + Spacebar + 5
Sample Weight (Weight Paint Only)	Shift + Spacebar + 6
Sample Vertex Group (Weight Paint Only)	Shift + Spacebar + 7
Annotate	Shift + Spacebar + 5 (Weight) Shift + Spacebar + 8 (Vertex)
Annotate Line	Shift + Spacebar + 6 (Weight) Shift + Spacebar + 9 (Vertex)
Annotate Polygon	Shift + Spacebar + 7 (Weight) Shift + Spacebar + 0 (Vertex)
Annotate Eraser	Shift + Spacebar + 8 (Weight) Shift + Spacebar + Shift + 1 (Vertex)

APPENDIX B

Blender's History

Let's talk about Blender's history a little bit. Of course, we need to at least learn about the background of the software we are going to use, not just use it. In this way, we will know what the main feature of the software is, especially for this kind of software that has many features.

Blender 3D is a 3D suite software. It is a free and open source software. This means, by price, it is free and that its license is under the GNU General Public License.

Blender 3D started as an in-house software in NeoGeo, a Dutch animation studio of which Ton Roosendaal was a co-founder. It was started in 1995 when Ton decided to rewrite the current in-house software of the animation studio that had become one of the leading animation houses in Europe. At that time, Ton was responsible for both art direction and software development.

In 1998 a new company was developed named NaN (Not a Number) as a spin-off of NeoGeo to market and develop Blender for free; and in 1999, NaN attended its first SIGGRAPH convention and it was a huge success. In 2001, NaN restarted with new investor funding and after six months launched its first commercial software named Blender Publisher. Unfortunately, because of disappointing sales and the ongoing difficult economic climate, the new investors decided to shut down all NaN operations. This shutdown also included discontinuing the development of Blender. Even though there's a lot of shortcomings like unfinished features and complex internal software architecture, because of the enthusiastic support from the user community and customers who had purchased Blender Publisher, Ton could not justify leaving Blender and founded the nonprofit organization named Blender Foundation in March 2002.

Blender Foundation's primary goal was to find a way to continue to develop and market Blender as a community-based open source project and by October 13, 2002, Blender was released under the terms of the GNU GPL. The development of Blender continues up until now, together with its goal-driven team.

© Ezra Thess Mendoza Guevarra 2020
E. T. Mendoza Guevarra, *Creating Game Environments in Blender 3D*,
https://doi.org/10.1007/978-1-4842-6174-2

So, let me share you a little bit about the major development of Blender in each year, starting from its birth year, which was in 1994.

In 1998, an SGI version was published on the web and it was called IrisGL. The same year, Linux, FreeBSD, and Sun versions were released.

In 1999, Windows, BeOS, and PPC version were released.

In 2000, an Interactive 3D, real-time engine, physics, and Phyton were added to its features.

In 2001, a character animation system was added and the MacOs version was released.

In 2002, Blender goes open source.

In 2003, the first true open source version was released, and a preview was released of 2.3x UI makeover presented at the second Blender conference.

In 2004, a major overhaul of internal rendering capabilities was added, game engine returns, ambient inclusions, new procedural textures, particle interactions, and LSCM UV mappings were added, functional YafRay integration, weighted creases in subdivision surfaces, ramp shaders, and full OSA.

In 2005, a full rework of the armature system was done, shape keys, fur with particles, rigid bodies, soft bodies, force fields, deflections, incremental subdivisions surfaces, transparent shadows, and a multi-threaded rendering were added.

In 2006, nodes were released, an array modifier and vector blur were added, and a new physics engine.

In 2007, reawakening of the 64-bit OS support, and the addition of subsurface scattering, multi-resolution meshes, multilayer UV textures, multilayer images, multi-pass rendering and baking, retopology, sculpting, multiple mattes, distort and filter nodes, fluid particles, proxy objects, and post-production UV texturing.

In 2008, light and game engine improvements, GLSL shaders, snap, sky simulator, shrink-wrap modifier, a mesh deform modifier and action editor were added, enhanced image browsing, and integrated a seamless and nonintrusive physics cache.

In 2009, game engine enhancements included video textures where you can play movies in game, Boolean mesh operator improved, and node-based textures, armature sketching, JPEG2000 support, and projection painting for direct transfer of images to models were added.

And from 2009 to 2011, Blender was recoded – total refactor of the software with new functions on its version 2.5x.

In 2011, the internalization of the UI and the Cycles renderer, the camera tracker, the ocean modifier, and the dynamic paint for modifying textures with mesh contact/approximation were added.

In 2012, fire and smoke improvements and a carve library to improve Boolean operations, remesh modifier, ambient occlusion, viewport display of background images and render layers, mask editor, and anisotropic shader for Cycles were added.

In 2013, a better support for FBX import/export was develop, and Dynamic topology, rigid body simulation, freestyle, more modeling tools, and new add-ons for 3D printing were added.

In 2014, Cycle gets basic volumetric support on the CPU, deformation motion blur and fire/smoke support are added in Cycles, Cycles gets volume and subsurface scattering support on GPU, and pie menus, intersection modeling tool, and new sun beam mode for the Compositor were added.

In 2015, Improvement to hair dynamics was made and the support for custom normals, view compositing, Pixar open SubDiv support, node auto-offset, and a text-effect strip for the sequencer were added.

In 2016, OpenVDB support for caching of smoke/volumentric simulations develop, Cycles support for spherical stereo images for VR and Alembic import and export were added, Grease Pencil works became more similar to other 2D drawing software.

In 2017, new Cycles features added: denoising, shadow catcher, and new Principled shader.

In 2019, a totally redesigned UI for easier navigation and new features added, and this was Blender 2.80.

So, this is the short history of Blender. Let me discuss a little bit about its installation process for the readers who will use it for the first time.

Index

E. T. Mendoza Guevarra, *Creating Game Environments in Blender 3D*,
https://doi.org/10.1007/978-1-4842-6174-3

W

X, Y, Z

Printed in the United States
By Bookmasters